A WORD TO MY YOUNGER SELF

YOU ARE MORE THAN YOUR WORST MISTAKE

ISBN hardcover 9781945419676

ISBN softcover 9781945419607

ISBN ebook 9781945419614

Library of Congress Control Number 2020940222

100% of book proceeds benefit Epicenter Ministries

"When I was a child, I talked like a child, I thought like a child, I reasoned like a child. When I became an adult, I put the ways of childhood behind me."

1 Corinthians 13:11 (NET)

Dear Younger Me

Lyrics by MercyMe

Dear younger me
Where do I start
If I could tell you everything that
I have learned so far
Then you could be
One step ahead
Of all the painful memories still
running thru my head
I wonder how much different things
would be

Dear younger me,
Dear younger me
I cannot decide
Do I give some speech about how to
get the most out of your life
Or do I go deep
And try to change the choices that
you'll make 'cause they're choices
that made me
Even though I love this crazy life
Sometimes I wish it was a smoother
ride
Dear younger me, dear younger me
If I knew then what I know now
Condemnation would've had no
power
My joy my pain would've never
been
my worth

If I knew then what I know now
Would've not been hard to figure
out

What I would've changed if I had
heard
Dear younger me
It's not your fault
You were never meant to carry this
beyond the cross
Dear younger me
You are holy
You are righteous
You are one of the redeemed
Set apart a brand new heart
You are free indeed
Every mountain every valley
Thru each heartache you will see
Every moment brings you closer
To who you were meant to be
Dear younger me, dear younger
me

You are holy
You are righteous
You are one of the redeemed
Set apart a brand new heart
You are free indeed
You are holy
You are righteous
You are one of the redeemed
Set apart a brand new heart
You are free indeed
You are holy
You are righteous
You are one of the redeemed
Set apart a brand new heart
You are free indeed

FOREWORD

Many adults remember their teenage years as a time of lessons learned, opportunities revealed, and milestones reached. But for an unfortunate few, those same years were marked with trauma, abuse, impulsive mistakes, and harsh consequences. Whereas most feared detention or video game restrictions for their transgressions, many of us faced a lifetime in prison for ours. I often think back to that time in my own life and wonder, *what would I say to my 16-year-old self to prepare her for the journey that lies ahead?* It's a question I'm sure most ask themselves at one point in time or another. But for the individuals in *A Word to My Younger Self,* the answer is marked with a heavier tone than most. As you read the letters compiled here, I challenge you to think of what a letter to your younger self would say. And once you've read through this book, ask yourself the more challenging questions: What does it say about our country that our children are subjected to the things you read here? And, more important, what can *you* do to help change it?

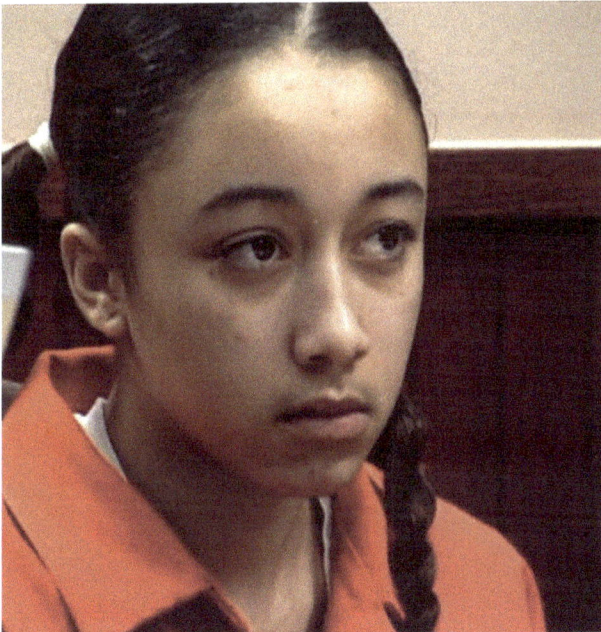

Dear Cyntoia,

God hears you. You've been crying out to Him for the past several weeks, begging Him to take control over the situation you're facing, and right now you're not sure that He even hears you. I wish I could tell you that you'll be able to see immediately that He has answered you, but unfortunately, God's timing doesn't work like that. On the contrary, a wild swing of events is about to take place that will cause you to question whether He even exists. But just keep your faith and trust me when I say – He hears you, and He will come through for you.

Your life has already taken a drastic turn in just the past few months, and although you may feel like you couldn't bear any more, you WILL make it! You are a survivor. You don't realize that yet, but you are so much bigger than anything that anyone tried to do to hurt you. You are a fighter. There is a fire that burns inside of you that will eat up any obstacle that dares to stand in your way. Many lonely nights lie ahead of you, many days when you feel that emptiness stretches out endlessly before you, but if you would only grit your teeth through these moments, you will see that your next breath is waiting for you just beyond the breaking point. Remember these things because you will need to constantly remind yourself of them over the next 15 years.

I know right now it seems like all you ever hear is talk of what a horrible person you are. They call you a whore, a murderer, incorrigible. But I want you to know that you are so much more than the worst thing that you've ever done. You won't find your value in your regrets, but in who the Lord made you to be. When He sees you, He sees so much more than your mistakes, so much more than your shortcomings – He sees a beautiful, intelligent young woman with so much to offer. When people try to bury you under your past, learn to see yourself as your Father in Heaven sees you.

You are about to go through many ups and downs. For starters, you'll be told that you are going to die in prison. You'll spend some time believing that the world is against you and that you may never be happy again. You'll be exploited and mistreated by people for years to come. And you'll have your hopes of freedom dashed repeatedly, each time beating your resolve more than the last. But as I said before: YOU WILL MAKE IT! It's important for you to remember that!

The lie about dying in prison? It's just that, a lie. Just when you thought God hadn't heard your prayer, He is going to show up in a way that is beyond your wildest imagination. You will learn that there are many people from all parts of the world who support you. Who believe in you. You will know once again that happiness is meant for you too! You WILL know happiness, Cyntoia! And through the people who mistreated you, you will know forgiveness. And it will give you a freedom that you can enjoy even in prison. Most important, though, you will forgive yourself. It will be hard, and it will take years, but you will love yourself again.

You can't see it now, but God is going to use you in a mighty way. Through you, He will give a voice to the voiceless. Once you are free, you will speak up at every opportunity to encourage justice, freedom, and mercy for the oppressed. And that prayer you prayed…the one where you promised to tell the world about God once He freed you? That will come to fruition as well. You'll one day get the chance to tell the world every detail of your journey through the system and how the Lord freed you from it all. Like I said, GOD HEARS YOU!

Cyntoia Brown Long was released from prison on August 7, 2019. She is the author of *Free Cyntoia: My Search for Redemption in the American Prison System*

CONTENTS

INTRODUCTION TO SECOND LOOK AT
THE TEXAS LEGISLATURE

It is wrong to deny a child the opportunity to demonstrate rehabilitation. However, in Texas, kids who are sentenced to an adult prison can be required to serve 40 years before even becoming *eligible* for parole; our laws currently provide no viable mechanism for reviewing a case after a young person has grown up and matured.

Tremendous growth and maturity often occur in a person's late teens through mid-20s, and research has shown that certain areas of the brain, particularly those that affect judgment and decision-making, do not fully develop until the early 20s.[1] The U.S. Supreme Court has acknowledged youths' ongoing development, stating in its 2005 *Roper v. Simmons* decision, "[t]he reality that juveniles still struggle to define their identity means it is less supportable to conclude that even a heinous crime committed by a juvenile is evidence of irretrievably depraved character."[2]

The fact that young adults are still developing means they are uniquely situated for personal growth and rehabilitation. In 2012, the U.S. Supreme Court held unconstitutional mandatory life without parole sentences for people under the age of 18, and required courts to consider the youthfulness of defendants facing that sentence.[3] This decision, coupled with the *Roper* decision, recognizes that it is wrong to deny someone who commits a crime under the age of 18 the opportunity to demonstrate rehabilitation. However, Texas sentencing laws ignore recent scientific evidence on adolescent development and neuroscience, and the state's current parole system provides no viable mechanism for reviewing a case after a young person has grown up and matured.

This is a very costly approach, both in terms of human capital and taxpayer dollars. It costs approximately $2.5 million to incarcerate a person for life, whereas it costs taxpayers approximately $625,720 to incarcerate a person for 20 years.[4] Texas law should motivate young people to focus on rehabilitation, and it should provide a path to redemption for those who can prove they merit a second chance. Early release for individuals who have demonstrated that they have sufficiently matured and rehabilitated can save the state approximately $1,874,280 per person[5].

Texas should consider joining with other states that have provided a "second look" at the sentences of individuals who were convicted for crimes committed prior to their 18th birthday. Texas could provide an early parole hearing focused on the extent to which the person has demonstrated that he or she has successfully rehabilitated and matured. Such an early parole consideration will not only save taxpayer dollars, it will do so without compromising public safety.

Given everything the U.S. Supreme Court has said about the inherent characteristics of adolescence, and with all of the backing scientific research that the Court considered across cases, a de facto life sentence is cruel and unusual, and is highly inappropriate for juveniles. It is time to return to the juvenile justice system's initial emphasis on rehabilitation – rather than the more punitive and misguided approach of the 1980s and 1990s – and ensure that the Texas Legislature establishes laws and practices in keeping with the spirit of the *Miller* and *Roper* decisions.

LINDSEY LINDER

SENIOR POLICY ATTORNEY, TEXAS CRIMINAL JUSTICE COALITION

AN INTRODUCTION TO TEXAS PAROLE

"2D – Nature of the Offense."

The Texas Board of Pardons and Paroles has a short list of codified reasons that they use to explain the reason for denying a person release on parole. Many of the people reading this book who entered prison as children – as well as their loved ones and advocates – will recognize "2D" as the Board's shorthand way of saying that a person simply has not done enough time by the Board's measure.[1]

As I write this, countless men and women are working diligently inside of prison walls, educating themselves in preparation for reentry to the workforce; devoting themselves to spiritual practices; and engaging in probing rehabilitative counseling programs in order to prepare for successful reentry. Without a change in our system, thousands of them will also come to know the hopeless feeling that many already know when they see the "2D" year after year, in spite of their efforts.

At the point of the "2D" vote, the purpose of incarceration is no longer rehabilitation, but oppression. Continue to live in sweltering Texas heat unmitigated by air conditioning.[2] Continue to work for free to produce the necessary items that your family will have to pay a premium to buy you.[3] Continue to live in an environment where you are at risk of being murdered by the public servants employed to ensure safety in the facility.[4] Have your life expectancy shortened by two years for each year that you remain incarcerated.[5]

Do these things, the government is saying, not because of your present conduct, but because of a decision you made as a child.

Indeed, youth at the time of the allegation is considered an aggravating factor in the Parole Guidelines scoring system, the rubric used by Parole Board Members and Commissioners to assess the risk associated with granting release.[6] Likewise, conditions inherent in children, such as lack of employment history prior to arrest and association with negative peer groups, are deemed to be indicative of higher risk.[7]

The Parole Guidelines Risk Assessment – a simple, one-page worksheet – was made in response to a legislative mandate to remedy decades of clandestine policy changes made to justify arbitrary decisions relating to release[8] amid an era of rampant civil rights violations that caused Texas's prison system to be placed into federal receivership.[9] Decades after the advent of the Parole Guidelines Score system, the Board is "not fully and consistently using the parole guidelines as intended," leading to inconsistent approval rates across parole panels reviewing individuals with comparable scores.[10]

Advances in how we understand human development reveal the obsolescence of the Parole Guidelines Score rubric. Modern psychology tells us that youth at the time of the allegation allows for greater capacity for rehabilitation.[11] Modern neuroscience tells us that the decisions that land a child in adult prison are a temporary condition of youth, resulting from a structurally immature brain that will ultimately grow to function in a way that is more rational and mature.[12]

In response to this understanding, the United States Supreme Court famously acknowledged the difference between children and adults, and that punishments which might pass constitutional muster for adults are cruel and unusual as applied to children.[13]

The language in these Supreme Court opinions continues to be aspirational from the vantage point of a practitioner, prisoner, or prisoner's loved one in Texas. To date, Texas's policy response has been to delegate to the Board of Pardons and Paroles the decision as to whether a child dies in prison. The flaw in that design is that the Texas parole review, as a system, fails to consider the mitigating qualities of youth. Candidates for parole who are paying for childhood mistakes are dependent upon the discretion of parole voters who choose to depart from their prescribed rubric.

In a system that views children who enter prison as inherently high risk, individual candidates pray to be seen as exceptional by a decision-making body that reviews 6,000 cases per month.[14] Candidates are not entitled to representation by counsel. Candidates are not entitled to a hearing.

As a practitioner who has looked into the eyes of many juvenile lifers, heard their stories, and investigated their histories for myself, I can tell you that the road to their fates are generally paved by some combination of heavy stone: pain and trauma; victimization and abuse; school and child welfare systems that failed them; and illnesses and disabilities beyond their control.

At present, there is no rubric accounting for what these men and women have been through. There is no rubric accounting for what measures these remarkable individuals are taking to overcome odds and persevere. Second Look calls for that type of comprehensive review.

The Second Look Bill[15] calls for the Board to consider myriad factors when reviewing candidates for parole who entered prison as children. Not only would review take into account the diminished capacity of juveniles and hallmark features of youth, but it would also take into account the candidate's own individual circumstances. Family history, prenatal history, developmental history, medical history, trauma history, and social history all become relevant factors in the parole review decision. Psychological evaluations will provide additional insight into the mental status of the individual.

Parole voters will be able to make meaningful decisions based upon the whole person, and not by obsolete and impersonal scoring instruments. Although detractors often suggest that Second Look's earlier eligibility date will release people they deem "dangerous" while they are still at risk to society, the opposite is true. Because of the more in-depth and individualized review of the candidate's history, voters will not only have a better view of the individuals who demonstrate growth and maturity, but also those who do not.

If anything, a more meaningful parole review makes society safer without erring on the side of condemning children to die in prison in the name of public safety. Especially people who are – as I write and as you read – toiling to overcome obstacles that many never survive. There are examples of strength and courage within those walls from which we all can learn.

"2D" cannot be the sole factor in determining whether a child dies in prison. Because "[e]ach of us is more than the worst thing we've ever done."[16]

CHRIS SELF

PROFESSOR – JUVENILE LIFERS EXTERNSHIP PROGRAM THURGOOD MARSHALL SCHOOL OF LAW

CHIEF COUNSEL, EPICENTER MINISTRIES

JUVENILES & THE LAW OF PARTIES
HOW THE PERVASIVENESS OF PEER PRESSURE, LACK OF FUTURE ORIENTATION, AND DEVELOPING MATURITY INTERACT TO CREATE 'THE PERFECT STORM'

Understanding the Law of Parties requires a discussion of the law, as well as social and scientific factors. Each factor plays a critical role in determining an individual's association with another; especially when the individual is a juvenile.

The Law of Parties provides that one individual can be held criminally liable for actions committed by another. The Texas Penal Code considers each participant to a crime, a "party," and thus, criminally responsible for the offense committed.[1] There are various circumstances in which a person is criminally responsible for an offense committed by the conduct of another. The Texas Penal Code describes them as: (1) causing or helping an innocent person to engage in criminal activity;[2] (2) intentionally promoting, helping, directing, encouraging, or soliciting another to commit a crime;[3] or (3) purposely assisting in the commission of, or failing to make a reasonable attempt to stop the occurrence of a crime one has a legal duty to prevent.[4]

I. Adolescents are more vulnerable to peer pressure and social influence

Children are the by-product of their environment: social interactions with peers and a desire to conform to a group identity significantly impact adolescent decision-making. Therefore, it is not uncommon (or surprising) for many adolescents to find themselves entangled in the criminal justice system as parties to an offense. The Supreme Court has recognized children are more vulnerable to negative influences and outside pressures...and lack the ability to extricate themselves from horrific, crime-producing settings.[5] This recognition in the law is supported by neuro-scientific studies, stating the effects of peer pressure are stronger during adolescence than in adulthood.[6] While adolescents and adults are similar in their ability to understand a situation's risk, the distinction lies in how they evaluate risks and rewards.[7] In particular, the developing adolescent brain is prone to seek peer approval (particularly in group settings) above many other rewards, and a fear of rejection influences their decisions.[8] Moreover, during puberty, adolescents increasingly interact with their peers more than with adults; reducing the influence an adult may have on how a child may develop their decision-making skills.[9] A child's increasing autonomy from their parents throughout adolescence compounds their susceptibility to peer pressure, specifically in situations involving pressure to engage in antisocial behavior.[10]

II. Developmental immaturity underscores the makeup of the adolescent brain

A hallmark of adolescent development is ongoing neurological maturation. Chemical and neurological influences greatly affect adolescent behavior. Brain imaging studies illustrate the increase in neural reactivity in the areas of the brain that promote risky behavior.[11] The lack of judgmental maturity in adolescent brains highlights the key difference between adult and adolescent brains.[12] However, the significance of the studies is not finding the immaturity of a younger brain, but rather, that a child's brain develops. Over time, the brain's structure and functions change, specifically in areas contributing to thoughts, actions, and emotions.[13] Importantly, there is an opportunity for growth in the adolescent brain: both physically and mentally. Additionally, logical decision-making is a skill children develop throughout their adolescence. Often, the learning curve can be difficult as adolescents experience fluctuating emotions and lack an adult's capacity to resist reckless behavior, risk-taking, and sensation seeking.[14] During puberty, adolescents experience a rapid increase in sensation-seeking behavior.[15] The tendency toward such behavior increases the adolescent's susceptibility to become ensnared in the juvenile or criminal justice systems as a party to an offense.

III. 'Future Orientation' is an ability indicative of age and maturation

A distinctive characteristic of adolescence is a lack of future orientation: the degree to which an individual considers the future, the ability to plan future goals, and anticipate future consequences.[16] Compared with adults, adolescents are more likely to focus on their current circumstances rather than long-term consequences. It has been suggested that this focus on the 'here and now' makes adolescents more likely to make choices that have a negative impact on their long-term health and well-being.[17] Moreover, throughout adolescence, children seek both emotional and decision-making independence from their parents. While these are necessary developmental changes, they have also been considered potential explanations for the concurrent rise in involvement in some risk behaviors that occur during adolescence.[18] Further, research shows that teens who engage in certain types of antisocial behavior may enjoy higher status among their peers as a consequence, perhaps because they appear to be independent of adult authority.[19] The short-range desirability of such status leads adolescents to engage in antisocial behaviors that they will soon outgrow.

A child engaging in negative social behavior does not imply the child will *always* exhibit such behavior. More important, it does not guarantee that the child will recede as an adult: adolescents are not destined for a life of criminal behavior. It has been noted that skill-building interventions focusing on cognitive-behavioral techniques, social skills, and academic and vocational skill-building can reduce juvenile recidivism rates.[20] Moreover, in-detention academic achievement has shown to reduce the risk of a child receding.[21] Our understanding that a child's developing maturity impacts their reasoning and decision-making is supported by science. Adolescents are more prone to seek immediate gratification and are less risk-averse than adults, as the parts of an adolescent brain that influence pleasure-seeking and emotional reactivity develop faster than those which support self-control. This developmental immaturity directly impacts the decisions children make about participating in more risky behavior. The susceptibility to peer pressure is highest during mid-adolescence, and conformity is greater when the behavior is antisocial.[22] Children are likely to engage in risky behavior in order to conform to a group identity and are, subsequently, more likely to be sentenced under the Law of Parties. However, just as neurological maturity is an indication of necessary development into adulthood, so, too, is the decrease in social pressure, in adults, to engage in risky behavior. An adolescent brain is always developing. As one individual is developing, so, too, is their social environment, which is likely made up of their peers, experiencing the same development. Social and mental maturation is a key factor in recognizing that adolescents have a greater capacity for rehabilitation than adults.

Such maturation occurs long before Second Lookers become eligible for release. As such, children are more than one undesirable act and in fact, are capable of so much more.

Jasmine Bond

Parole Attorney

Private Practice and Epicenter Ministries

Lindsay West

Student – Juvenile Lifers Externship Program

Thurgood Marshall School of Law

Expected J.D.: Spring 2021

1

JERMAINE HICKS

Hi, my name is Jermaine Hicks. I have been incarcerated since the age of 15 as a Law of Parties case, charged with capital murder. It wasn't until I let go of childhood anger that I started to reflect on my life and the lives of others. Under current legislation, I won't be eligible for parole review until I've served 40 years, which will be in 2034. My vision is to be released from prison and become the true leader in my community, which God has planned me to be.

Jermaine,

I compose my thoughts to you this day in hopes that you internalize them into a consciousness that will allow you to see the world in full view. Because without argument, the way you process this information will determine your circumstances. I pray that you consume every word knowing that I speak to you in love, care, and an understanding you have yet to comprehend, but you will.

The first thing I would like to tell you is this: I acknowledge all of those emotions you have built up inside your core and tend to release in ways that only hurt you even more. I understand that the reason for that pain is not in your control. The world around you has shaped physical images and situations that affect you. I realize also that you have allowed these images and your circumstances to overtake your better judgment by not fully thinking about how your reactions to life's actions can cause you damage; damage to the degree of losing your sense of self and your freedoms.

I know you wish things could be different. Being taken away from your mother, and your father going to prison, are traumatizing effects on a child of five years old. I know you never developed a sense of true love in those foster homes. So, as you grew, you embraced an artificial love that had no positive or beneficial substance that could have allowed you to grow. Becoming a gang member will not allow you to develop that love. Life is taking you fast, but if you slow down and see what's important, you will find the steps you must take to change your circumstances. Your father is uneducated. He cannot read or write well enough to teach you. You must learn how to find an interest in books and stop being afraid to ask for help. If you learn how to read, it will open up your mind to so much information. This information will change your perspective toward your environment in a way that could lead you to help your community and not hurt it. You will find yourself in a leadership role for productive change.

Understand that mistakes do not define who you are. You can be resilient. Time waits for no one. So, you must make a choice. Don't have any fear. Challenge yourself because it will help you help others, as well as learn how to deal with adversity. Know your worth. Know that one day you will be a man with many responsibilities. Even though I know you regret your mistakes, I'm not mad at you because it made me the man I am today.

Respectfully spoken,

ACCOMPLISHMENTS

- **Education:** GED (Windham School District), on the waiting list for college
- **Programs/Certificates:** Cognitive Intervention, The Horizon Program, Bridges to Life (Facilitator), Toastmasters International (Phoenix Gavel Club), Redefining Manhood
- **Work/On-the-Job Training:** Custodial Technician
- **Other:** Published in the Second Look book, volunteer with SOLC Transformation Fellowship, creator and co-editor of *Resilient News* (newsletter for the Giddings State School), creator of Redefining Manhood (gang prevention program for youths and young adults), Epicenter Advisory Board, Epicenter Unit Leader

2

SHAINA SEPULVADO

My name is Shaina Sepulvado. In 2005, at age 16, I was given a life sentence. I've been incarcerated for 14 years and am currently 30 years old. I'm eligible for parole in 2045.

Dear 16-year-old Shaina,

I know all the hurt you've been through feels like an excuse to be wild and rebellious, but you have no idea how precious life is. You think because you've never had a speeding ticket you can never be one of those people who go to jail or prison. Never say "never."

You don't like to be told what to do and you think, "I do the same thing every day with the same people. What harm could come to me?" Yet little do you know, all it takes is one slip, one mistake, and your whole life is gone.

You are living a life filled with drugs, drinking, and boys. While you feel like this is living, you are wrong. None of those things ultimately care about you in the end.

As time goes by, you'll realize there were many people you didn't listen to that you should have. Right now, you feel like people who claim to love you will always steer you in the right direction, but that is not true.

Not all love is good love, not all love is pure. People use love to manipulate you into doing things their way. Open your eyes, because those same people won't be there in the end. Your family will be the first to turn on you.

I've been sitting in prison for 15 years. Every day I wish someone would have helped save me. I lost my whole life behind "a night of fun." I wanted so many things out of life, but this prison wasn't one of them. I was rebellious and wouldn't listen to anyone. I thought I knew everything, yet I knew nothing.

Everyone goes through pain and sorrow. Nobody is exempt from that. However, it doesn't give you the right to hurt others. The fact that "hurt people hurt people" doesn't make it right.

I'm the one who lost in the end.

My life should have meant more to me than all of that. I've paid for my slip-up every day since that one night. I can't get a do-over, but you can take my advice and learn from my bad choices. I am in constant regret over my poor choices. Live your life to the fullest, take advantage of your freedom and make something of yourself. Do what I didn't do and live.

Love,

Shaina Sepulvado

ACCOMPLISHMENTS

- **Education:** GED (Windham School District), various college classes including Physical Geology
- **Work/On-the-Job Training:** Cook, Baker
- **Other:** Field Squad

3

KESEY DARNELL FRANK

My name is Kesey Darnell Frank. I was once a misguided individual out of millions worldwide, searching for love and acceptance in all of the wrong places. This led to my incarceration at the tender age of 17 (2002), and eventually receiving a life sentence in December 2003, with no parole in sight until 2042. I've been incarcerated for almost 18 years.

"In the name of GOD, the all-compassionate, the all-merciful." *The Qu'ran 1:1*

"Do you not see how GOD makes a metaphor of a good word: a good tree whose roots are firm and whose branches are in heaven? It bears fruit regularly by its LORD's permission. GOD makes metaphors for people so that, HOPEFULLY, they will pay heed. The metaphor of a corrupt word is that of a rotten tree, uprooted on the surface of the earth. It has no staying power. GOD makes those who believe firm with the FIRM WORD in the life of this world and Hereafter." *The Qu'ran 14:24-27*

Kesey,

I hope and pray for God's all-compassionate peace and unending blessings be upon you, your family (who loves you), and all of those courageous people who stand beside you. Forever!

Looking back, I knew that those words (above) from the Quran went way over your head. You could not fathom them at all. And Kesey, that's okay. Because life is NEVER meant for us to grasp EVERY-THING in one sitting (that's unrealistic for anyone). No, life is like the metamorphosis of becoming a beautiful butterfly: first, you must crawl upon earth's surface through the mud, through all of the filth and pain by stepping over each stone and hurdle, climbing over EVERY mountaintop, until you finally reach that life-giving FREEDOM tree, in which to build your cocoon, called "mental and spiritual maturity."

And I'm here telling you NOW! You have reached THAT TREE to shed the protective "incubative" cocoon to spread your GOD-given BEAUTIFUL wings of love, knowledge, wisdom, and understanding for not only yourself but for others just like you.

Just continue to fly higher and higher, knowing that the only one who can stop you is "YOU."

I love you, Kesey! GOD and Crystal do too! Sincerely your friend,

Kesey D. Frank

P.S. Your life is valuable. ALL LIFE IS VALUABLE! Yet, the ones you ARE allowing to lead you don't value "you" at all.

ACCOMPLISHMENTS

- **Education:** GED (Windham School District), Carpentry Vocation, Computer Information Technology Vocation
- **Programs/Certificates:** Peer to Peer Education, Cognitive Intervention, Peer Health, Voyager, Overcomers, Faith-Based Dorm, Criminon Programs
- **Work/On-the-Job Training:** Garment Factory, Cook Prep, Chapel Sound Tech, Auto Technician

4

JASON ISAIAH ROBINSON

My name is Jason Robinson and I am 42 years old. I was born in Germany and moved to Killeen at the age of nine. I was convicted under the Law of Parties and have been incarcerated for 26 years. Under current legislation, I won't be eligible for parole until 2034. As I look back upon my life, I see many mistakes that I made. I know I hurt people and that's something I have to live with. If I could go back I would change it all.

Jay,

You're going to find it extremely hard to believe that this letter is from you, 25 years into the future, but you are the author, and these are your words, from a different time in life. You're 16 years old, and for the past few years, your life has been spiraling out of control. You haven't reached the point where you can admit that to others, but you're not so blind that you can't see the proof of that for yourself. You try to excuse your actions by telling yourself you're just going through some type of phase. But your excuses are only delaying you from dealing with the real problems behind all of this madness.

As each day passes, you continue to make one bad decision after another. What you fail to realize is eventually these bad decisions will add up, and the sum of these decisions will cost more than you could imagine. What's even worse, the price for all your poor choices will spill over into the lives of other people, and all of you will have to live with the burden of your mistakes.

I wish I could grab you right now, shake you, and sit your butt down! Once I knew I had your attention, I would describe to you what the next 25 years of our life will be like. But unfortunately, you're beyond my reach, and I can't warn you of all the pitfalls, or share with you the wisdom that comes with the experiences of life.

God knows how badly I wish I could talk to you right now. As I look back at you, it's hard for me to understand how you didn't see all of this coming. At 16, you're already a drug addict. Isn't that what you said wouldn't happen when you first started using drugs? You recently started your sophomore year of high school, yet you skip school so much, you're always behind. Where do you think you're headed in life? Do you remember all of those dreams you had for yourself? What happened to those ambitions? Can't you see the further you get away from those dreams, the more willing you're becoming to accept less from yourself? It shows in your attitude and your actions. You act like you don't care, but how could you not care about your life?

The truth is, you're just running from your problems, but what you fail to realize is you can't run from your problems. You either deal with them, or you end up creating new ones. You think this life is yours to live, but that's a very selfish way of thinking, and because of your selfish decisions, you will reap a lifetime worth of guilt, that I'll have to live with once you're long gone. I wish you realized that you have the power to rise above your circumstances. Life for everyone would be so different. You are throwing away our future before we have a chance to live. It didn't have to be like this. Living in prison wasn't our destiny.

You've Been Forgiven,

ACCOMPLISHMENTS

- **Education:** GED (Windham School District), A.A., Business Administration and Management (Lee College), A.A., Liberal Arts (Lee College)
- **Programs/Certificates:** Paralegal Certificate (Blackstone Institution), Automotive Specialization in Steering and Suspension (Windham School District), Peer Education, Changes, Bridges to Life
- **Work/On-the-Job Training:** Painter, Laundry, Kitchen, Janitor, Processing Plant, Law Library Clerk

5

FRANZ SUAZO

My name is Franz Giovanni Suazo. I was born in the Philippines, but my family moved to Houston, Texas, when I was 12 years old, after my father died of cirrhosis of the liver. At the age of 16, I was incarcerated for murder and attempted murder (gang-related case). I was sentenced to 55 years. I have been incarcerated for 26 years and will be seeing parole in 2021. I am going to be 42 years old on September 11, 2020.

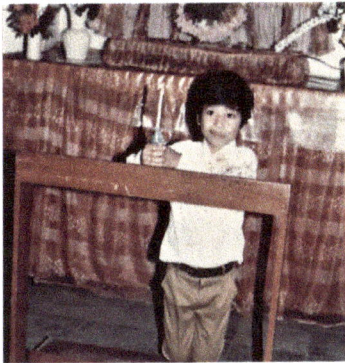

Dear Young Franz,

At this point in your life, you have been in a gang for quite a while. You have also been friends with some of these dudes a little longer than others. They are your close friends that you grew up with, and nobody can convince you to stop hanging out with them for any reason. Your family and teachers in school tell you that you are going down the wrong path because you are going in and out of the juvenile detention center.

You're angry, alone, and in pain, because nobody seems to understand you. When you do tell somebody, nobody knows what to do. It hurts you to be reminded that you do not have a father to talk to, or just hang out with and play catch. Your friends in the gang seem to be the only ones who understand you and also have the answers to temporarily ease your pain and loneliness. They always have your back. And because of that, you are obligated to lay down your life for their friendship.

Franz, I am here to tell you that the gang and the world you decided to create among your gang-related friends are the cause of your anger, pain, and loneliness. The longer you commit yourself to this crazy world, the more you believe all the lies the gang life offers you. You will lose touch with reality and lose sight of your real identity. You always have your own family that loves you and supports you, but you shut them out. Your family's love for you outdoes the deceiving love your gang friends have for you. It's not hard to figure out that your gang friends always manage to have you in the front of every gang fight, or be in a hangout spot that always ends up getting shot up. That alone will prove that you are now just a pawn they use to do whatever with.

Their enemies are now your enemies even if that enemy is one of your friends or family members. You are now bound by their own rules and stupidity, while they take advantage of your loyalty. You are not the only kid that ever went through the things you are going through. You know other kids that are going through these obstacles and have gone through worse but still manage to keep their life in a straight path. You are friends with some of those kids who have no family support.

You are not alone, and you can survive this crazy stage of your life. You have your siblings that will be there for you and your real friends that don't like to see you get in front of harm. Start a new direction and leave that gang life alone. The adversity you will go through of cutting your gang friends off is not as bad as being dead on the sidewalk with a bullet in your head, or a 55-year sentence in prison. A woman once said, "If you want a place in the sun, you've got to put up with a few blisters" (Abigail Van Buren). Make new friends and ask God to help you with your new journey.

Sincerely,

ACCOMPLISHMENTS

- **Education:** B.S. Behavioral Science (University of Houston, In Progress), A.A. Liberal Arts (Trinity Valley Community College), Auto-Mechanic College Trade (Lamar College)
- **Programs/Certificates:** Kairos, Acts, Bridges to Life
- **Work/On-the-Job Training:** Electrical Technician, Plumbing Technician, Welder, Barber, Warehouse Clerk, Invoice Control Clerk, General Clerk, Locksmith Technician

6

DEON LASHUN WILLIAMS

My name is Deon Williams. In 1993, at the tender age of 16 years old, I was convicted of first-degree murder under the Law of Parties and sentenced to 60 years in TDCJ. I've been incarcerated for over 26 years. I'm 42 years old now and will be 46 years old when I'm eligible for parole for the very first time in 2024.

Deon,

You have to stop being so hard-headed and disobedient. Mama only gets onto you because she's telling you what's best for you. Look at your big brother Edward: Do you want to be like him going in and out of juvenile detention centers and jails? Man, you must understand there is a price you have to pay for seemingly simple choices.

I know you may feel the world is against you, but that's not true. I can assure you that there are people in the world who are going through worse things in life than you are. You have a clean place to stay and although you can't afford all the name-brand clothes and shoes, you still have new clothes and shoes to wear. Learn to be thankful and grateful for what you are blessed to have. Don't be materialistic. You are young, smart, and have the potential for much success in life.

I know it's hard to concentrate in school when you have people that are more fortunate than you laugh and joke about how you are dressed, but that's okay. Deon, take the high road, overlook their foolishness. I know it's hard, but you can do it. I have faith in you. The hurt will only last as long as you allow it. You are in control of your own destiny. Never allow someone to have control of you or your thoughts. There will be obstacles put in your path, but your job will be to fight through them and rise above your adversity.

Even though you wished for better role models to look up to, know that they were there. You just didn't know what to look for. That is okay because you will make it. Grandmama Dorothy was there in your corner to point you toward a productive and successful life, if only you had taken the blinders away from your eyes.

You were afraid to show the interest that was in your heart and mind because you cared about what other people would say about you. Deon, don't worry if people don't accept you for being different or choosing not to indulge in drinking or smoking. They are not the definition of a real friend anyway. A real friend wants to see you accomplish your goals and succeed in a life of freedom and opportunity, not the life of incarceration. Sadly, incarceration is where you're headed if you don't straighten your act up.

Deon, you can accomplish goals on many levels, so take advantage of the opportunities that come your way. These will develop you into the man you've always dreamed of becoming. Work hard for whatever you want in life, and no matter what you choose to do, be the best at it. You never have to take anything from anyone.

When things don't go according to your plans, don't be discouraged. Instead, think of another alternative and keep striving forward. Remember: Be kind, for everyone you meet is fighting a battle you know nothing about.

Good luck to you,

Deon Willis

ACCOMPLISHMENTS

- **Education:** GED (Windham School District)
- **Programs/Certificates:** Operation Rebound, Anger Management, Computer-Aided Drafting, Computer Information Technology
- **Work:** Butcher, Baker, Cook, Janitor, Administration Segregation Janitor, Material Handler, Stock Clerk, Warehouseman, Leather Craftsman , Meat Packager, Butcher/Rendering Machine Operator, Food Service, Food Service Store Room Clerk
- **Other:** Field Squad, Epicenter Unit Leader

7

CHON PATRICK DIMAS

My name is Chon Patrick Dimas. Incarcerated days after my 17th birthday in 1998, I was convicted of first-degree murder and punished as an adult with a 75-year sentence and sent into the adult prison system. Now 39 years old, I have been incarcerated going on 22 years. Under current legislation, I will not be eligible for parole until I have served a minimum of 30 calendar years, which will be in 2028, when I am 47 years old.

Chon,

You may not know me, but I know you. I used to be just like you. You look at life through a kaleidoscope of negative emotions, some of which you carry on the surface, but others you hold repressively deep. It is well said that tomorrow is what we make of it, but the same can be said of yesterday. What we make of our days depends on how we view them, so our perception of events and circumstances is crucial in setting the course of our life.

You must change the way you see yourself, others, and life in general, especially concerning the past. Sometimes, we may gain a clearer or fuller view of something by looking at it from a distance. Try to take a step or two back from yourself and look at life through the lens of an outside-in rather than your normal inside-out scope. If you continue to internalize everything, you will misinterpret much about life and you will miss the bigger, more accurate picture. Tomorrow, if you approach life emotionally charged with your skewed perspective, no matter how swiftly the moment comes and goes, you will not bear the crucible of negative emotionality to come.

At age 17, little of what you think and feel is true. I know your type well. You erect defensive walls to protect against pain and disappointment. You think it's safer behind your walls, but barriers built to keep trauma out also means keeping past trauma in, and the longer it's in, the deeper it sinks down.

As former chief architect, I know walls like yours – thick and suffocating. Although you appear to breathe in everything so well, you gulp for air, but no one hears you panting on the verge of hyperventilation. Plus, you sometimes tend to hold your breath, and it's not healthy to build up a forceful release. You must learn to breathe in and breathe out. Tomorrow, if you confront life emotionally asphyxiated, your senses will be dulled and you will grasp for breath in a violently regretful way.

Every conflict we face, whether internally or externally, leads us to a pivotal position, even though we don't always realize it. Most people approach conflict on autopilot and react with impulsive emotionality or quick instinct. Don't be driven by your emotions. Don't react to conflict. Take time to think about what you may feel when emotions flare. Respond to conflict. There is a difference between reacting and responding.

Reacting neglects consideration of the risky consequences of your actions and usually abandons reason for the sake of emotional self-gratification.

Responding involves contemplating rational solutions in your mind rather than your heart.

While you have the gift of choice, use it wisely because one poor reaction may result in its forfeiture. Trust your senses over your emotions. You don't want to end up on the wrong side of the pivot point. If you're ever in doubt about a situation or feeling, call a friend. You are never as alone as you usually think you are. Trust me, there are people in your life who care about you, so stop isolating yourself. God didn't create us to be alone, and as poet John Donne reminds us, "No man is an island."

Tomorrow, you will be infused with strong emotions from some of your worst yesterdays. In a single moment of confrontation, everyone who ever hurt your mom will embody a single person and all their abusive acts will enliven a single threat to her life. Whatever Joyce screams at your mom, don't react to it because chances are she probably won't mean it. If you react, no matter how well-intentioned, you'll turn Joyce into a scapegoat and a victim, and she won't deserve it.

Tomorrow will be a day of strong emotion, but it will be a day of choice. From here on out, take time to think before you act. Breathe in, breathe out. Pray.

From one who has been there and done it,

Chon Dimas

ACCOMPLISHMENTS

- **Education:** M.A., Christian Education (Shalom Bible College & Seminary), M.A., Literature (University of Houston-Clear Lake), B.S., Behavioral Science (University of Houston-Clear Lake), A.A., General Liberal Arts (Alvin Community College), GED (Windham School District), College Vocational Trade in Computer Repair Technology (Alvin Community College)
- **Programs/Certificates:** Steps to Maturity, New Life Behavior Ministries Correspondence Courses (Managing My Anger, Attitudes & Behaviors, Christians Against Substance Abuse, A Sense of Self), Quest for Authentic Manhood, Houses of Healing (Emotional Intelligence), Peace Education, Alpha I & III (Participant and Mentor/Peer Facilitator), Voyager, Marriage & Parenting, Men's Fraternity, Anger Management, Bridges to Life (Participant and Encourager/Peer Facilitator), Overcomers, Peer Health & Sexual Assault Awareness, Cognitive Intervention, Youthful Offender Program
- **Work/On-the-Job Training:** Forklift Safety & Operation, OSHA General Industry Safety, General Clerk (Mechanical Department-Manufacturing, Agribusiness & Logistics Division), Laundry (Janitor, Stores Laborer, Warehouseman, General Clerk, Drying Machine Operator, All-Around Presser, Stock Control Clerk, Office Clerk, Necessities Clerk, Clothing Exchanger/Issuer, Washing Machine Operator), Offender Property Office Clerk, Agriculture, Food Service Department (Officer Dining Room, Kitchen Helper, Kitchen Commissary Clerk), Law Library Clerk
- **Other:** International Honor Society for English Literature Sigma Tau Delta (University of Houston-Clear Lake, Rho Omega Chapter), Epicenter Advisory Board

8

BRYAN O'NEIL COMER

M y name is Bryan Comer. At the age of 16, I was charged with two counts of capital murder. Being found guilty of both counts and given two life sentences, the judge ruled that they run concurrently. I have served 34 years and am now 50 years old. I am under the 1/3 law (1977-1987) which meant I only had to do 20 years to be eligible for parole. Since seeing parole for the first time in 2006, I have been set off five times in three- to five- year increments.

Dear Younger Self,

Slow down. There is more to life than what is going on at this moment. Think about what you truly want in life. Set goals and work hard to obtain them. Study hard in school to be successful and have a good life.

Make smart choices, think hard before you take any action, not only of how it affects you, but how it may affect others. Never be selfish and don't think only of yourself. Any action that you may take without really thinking all the way through can have adverse effects on others or you for the rest of your life!

Be careful about the people with whom you choose to be friends. Always be yourself, never be a follower. Choose good people who go to church and strive to live by God's teachings.

Value every moment you have with your parents. They are your very best friends in this world. No one else cares and loves you more than they do. You should mind and listen to everything they tell you. I sure wish I had done so.

Never make the mistake of doing drugs or hang around people who use them. People who get you to try drugs are not your friends at all. They will only use you, then abandon you in the end!

You should respect and cherish life. Surely, the lives of others. Never take anyone or anything in life for granted.

Sincerely,

Bryan Comer

ACCOMPLISHMENTS

- **Education:** GED (Windham School District), Auto Body Vocation (Trinity Valley College and Windham Auto Body)
- **Programs/Certificates:** Bridges to Life, Voyager, Experiencing God, Faith-Based Dorm, Overcomers, Recovery, Business Computer Information Systems, Anger Management, Substance Abuse, Cognitive Intervention, Gang Renouncement and Disassociation
- **Work/On-the-Job Training:** Assembly Fabrication, Metal Fabrication, Hydraulics Department, Welding, Furniture Factory
- **Other:** Published in *The Christian Ranchman*

9

FREDRICK ALEXANDER

My name is Fredrick Alexander, and I was incarcerated at 17 years old in 1995. I was sentenced to 99 years for first-degree murder and given two 20-year sentences for two aggravated assaults with a deadly weapon. I have been incarcerated for the last 24 years and counting. The first time I will be eligible for parole review is in 2025. By that point, I would have served 30 calendar years and be 47 years old.

Dear Fredrick,

I know you never thought a moment like this would ever come to be. However, it has arrived.

First, I want to apologize to you for the life I have led you to live and the decisions that you've made along the way.

I wish I could turn back the hands of time and forewarn you about the life-changing mistakes you would make in your future. I know now that growing up in a toxic environment was extremely detrimental. It led you to seek acceptance from crowds and people who meant you no good.

This caused you to fall victim to the peer pressures around you as a child. Looking back, I understand this was virtually inevitable because everything you witnessed and were taught growing up was detrimental. You were subjected to seeing and experiencing things no child should ever face.

I wish I could share with you back then some of what I know now. You deserved love and guidance within a healthy upbringing. Through love and proper guidance, you would have learned the importance of education and gained all the keys to life. One must be equipped at an early age with the knowledge of self to make more rational decisions.

Of course, the realities of all that were certainly different.

For at 17 years old, you had no clue that at 42 years old, you would be incarcerated for a dumb act of impulsive thinking. Something that lasted mere seconds has caused a ripple effect harming lives on many levels for the next 24 years and counting – the remainder of your life.

Heartbreaking, but true.

I wish there was a way to right the wrongs that led to this moment, although that's impossible on the physical plane. There is still much you can do. God works in mysterious ways. Thus, He has a plan and purpose for you just as He does all others.

Therefore, know that your biggest mistakes in life do not define who you are nor the person you can become.

For your journey continues.

"P.E.A.C.E."

ACCOMPLISHMENTS

- **Education:** GED (Windham School District), on the waiting list for college
- **Programs/Certificates:** AA, NA, Anger Management, College Prep, Purpose Driven Life, Think Tank "Raising Future Generations," Walk by Faith (Empowerment Course), on the waiting list for Bridges to Life, Voyager, Malachi Dads, Authentic Manhood, ROD Class, Disciple Class
- **Work/On-the-Job Training:** Garment Factory, Janitor Services, on the waiting list for Construction Carpentry

10

JUAN GUADALUPE GARCIA

M y name is Juan G. Garcia. I've been incarcerated since the age of 15, for an incident that occurred on August 14, 2008. I am serving a life sentence with the possibility of parole. I have been incarcerated for 12 years and am now 27 years old. Under current legislation, I'll be eligible for parole 2038.

Dear Juan,

I hope and pray that you read this letter carefully as I touch base on some of life's challenging experiences. I understand that you have been through a lot at such a young age. I can honestly say that I have faced some enduring obstacles in my life as well.

You will come across obstacles in your life – fair and unfair. You will discover, time and time again, that what matters most is not what these obstacles are, but how we see them, how we react to them, and whether we keep our composure. You will learn that this reaction determines how successful we will be in overcoming or possibly thriving because of them.

I know how it feels – to feel guilty, confused, defeated, depressed, suicidal, and to have many sleepless nights. I know how it feels to have nobody who understands what you are going through. When I lost my parents, I lost a sense of guidance. I was only 14.

I began to hang around the wrong crowd using drugs and drinking. I suppressed all the hurt and pain inside. Later, it emerged through my change of behavior. Little brother, you are only one choice from living a totally different life. It took me years to forgive myself and those who afflicted me. Forgiveness isn't an easy process. It's an everyday challenge. Drugs and alcohol only cover the wounds but in reality, when the feel-good sensation is gone, you find yourself in the same state of mind. Stay sober-minded!

As I hung around my peers. I felt like I had to prove myself to others and put on this tough persona. I was in an identity crisis. I didn't know who I was. I had a false sense of self. If you want to know where you are headed in life, look at your friends – the company you have around you. If they're not going places – stuck in the same mess – then chances are you won't get anywhere. Bad company corrupts good character.

You have many choices you will have to make in life. When you have to make a choice and don't make it, that's a choice in itself. Reject passivity, accept responsibility, lead courageously, and invest eternally, little brother.

I want to encourage you to keep pressing forward. I want to see you overcome these obstacles. Transmute this life of mess you have into a message for others. All the tests you experience will be your testimony to the world.

Sincerely yours,

Juan Garcia

ACCOMPLISHMENTS

- **Education:** GED (Windham School District)
- **Programs/Certificates:** Peer Health Education Course, Certificate of Excellent Achievement Award (Outstanding Performance and Accomplishment in Academics), Hermeneutics Class, Homiletics Class, Constructive Kingdom Men, Rite of Christian Initiation of Adults
- **Other:** Baptism

11

JAMES AARON DYSON

Hello! My name is James Aaron Dyson, but please call me Aaron. Shortly after my 17th birthday in 1997, I took the law into my own hands by shooting a man who murdered a childhood friend of mine. Following a speedy trial, I was sentenced to 50 years in prison as a first-time offender. I have been incarcerated for 22 years and am now 40 years old. I will be eligible for parole after completing 25 years, which will be January 6, 2023.

Aaron,

I was asked to reach into the past to write to you, to talk with you about the tale of two stories as your young life approaches a pivotal point in time. There is so much I would like to say to you. So much I would like to teach you. Above all else, I would love to take your hand and reintroduce you to Jesus. Considering you are of the past and I the present, such is patently impossible. At the very least, I can offer you words from my heart.

At this moment, you find yourself amid social trends offering misconceptions about life that will distract and misguide you if allowed. Make your way and follow your dreams, even when the path becomes difficult, because I assure you there is no barrier to what you can achieve. Take your time growing up because you will only experience adolescence once. Do not fret about the obstacles you have faced throughout your young life through learning disabilities and a speech impediment, nor the self-consciousness and humiliation it has generated, because it will all gradually fade away as your mind matures and grows. You will one day become a smart, well-spoken man. I promise you that. I encourage you to read everything because that will become instrumental in building your strengths of language and literacy, and will give you the power of expression. At times, it will enable you to touch others in unforgettable ways.

Learn to control your emotions and think things through. Always listen to your elders and never violate the law because there will be no way to undo the hardships and loss that will follow. Imprisonment strips away the ability to engage in life and causes a person to lose relationships with people they care for. It is something that resides in his consciousness; every single morning he wakes in the bowels of a smoldering hellhole of his making.

Always remain optimistic and keep a smile on your face, even during the moments when reasons to do so are tough to come by. Why? Because life is an immeasurable gift and not a second of it promised to anyone. You will encounter this harsh reality and the grief it causes as loved ones slip from this earth far too soon. I urge you to never leave emotions of love unexpressed because you may never be given another opportunity. I would like to share a metaphor with you from a book titled *Wrapped in Rain* by Charles Martin.

"You can't rake the rain, plow the clouds, or box up the sunshine, but, you can love."

These words left such an impression on me, conveying that things happen in life over which we have no control. The one thing we do have control over is the ability to love. We should do so freely and without restraint. Love others with everything you have, be quick to aid others when in need, protect those who need it, and always be willing to forgive those who have wronged you.

Be a blessing to others, always!

ACCOMPLISHMENTS

- **Education:** A.A.S., Small Business Management (Trinity Valley Community College), GED (Windham School District), College Vocations (Auto Body Repair, Construction Carpentry, Interior Trim & Cabinet Making, Small Business)
- **Programs/Certificates:** Cognitive Intervention, Voyager, Substance Abuse Educational Program, Anger Management, Stress Management, FEMA's Emergency Management Institute (Emergency Preparedness, Radiological Emergency Management, Animals in Disaster, Awareness & Preparedness, Community Planning), Livestock in Disaster, Leadership & Influence, Decision Making & Problem-Solving, Effective Communication, Radiological Emergency Response, The Professional in Emergency Management, High Honors Award (3.86 GPA)
- **Work/On-the-Job Training:** Broom Maker, Quality Technician
- **Other:** Phi Theta Kappa Honor Society (Iota Alpha Chapter, Trinity Valley College)

12

JEREMY GARTRELL

What's up, world? My name is Jeremy Gartrell. I am a sold out-servant-soldier of the Lord Jesus Christ. I was certified as an adult at 16 years old in 1994 and sentenced to 50 years in prison on October 23, 1995, at 17 years old. Today after nearly 25 years of incarceration, I am 41 years old and by the grace of God, recently received a favorable parole review on April 15, 2020. To God be the glory!

Jeremy,

I just wanted to share a poem I wrote for you titled, "Here I am Now."

> There was a time back in my young mind, gangsters to
>   me were "manhood" defined, up this mountain, I
>   started to climb,
> but at the base, I noticed a sign:
> "From here, only the strong will survive." Instantly this
>   fed into my pride,
> childhood anger, I couldn't hide,
> I thought this path was one where I'd thrive.
> I began to sense things were not right, no rocks, flowers,
>   or trees were in sight,
> chaos and violence reigned day and night, though I could
>   have left, I chose to fight.
> Fierce, determined, I charged to the peak, enticed by flesh
>   revealing I am weak,
> drugs, alcohol, and gangs made things bleak, engrossed
>   in lies, life started to reek.
> We all know pride goes before the fall, gorilla "big," yet I
>   was so small.
> Boom! One shot destroyed it all,
> straight from the mountain to behind a wall.
> Invincibility shattered, Hopes and dreams tattered,
> now I saw what really mattered,
> I'd been so blind, naive and battered.
> Fences and walls were all I could see,
> this wasn't how things were supposed to be, Al Capone
>   had been an idol for me,
> But then I was stuck and no longer free.
> The weight of deceit had crushed me breathless, It felt
>   like a nightmare – I was so restless.
> My quest for "manhood" had made me careless, A
>   murdered life rendered families helpless.
> Tears kept flowing from my mama's eyes, communities

shake when innocence dies, a man was severed from
his family ties.

this tragedy stemmed from heartache and lies.

Slowly the picture begins to fade, for this choice, a price
must be paid,

I looked to the sky, my soul now afraid, forever defined
by this mistake I had made.

But God…

He knew my heart like He knows every man, though
terribly tragic, it was part of His plan,

cops came to my home, throwing cuffs on my hands,
adrenaline drained, and I became deadpan.

A rescue mission ensued, such divine scale, but I felt like
a thug being buried in jail.

God sent the cops like He did Jonah's whale, I repented
and humbled myself while on bail.

In a small Baptist church, there was a head-on collision,
between this hard-headed thug and the Lord's perfect
vision, broken and wounded, I desired to be
Christian,

from thug life to eternal life, I finally made the decision.

God truly transformed me, I could tell, He saved me
from sin and the devil's hell,

though I'm incarcerated, I'm under no spell, like a Navy
Seal I'll never ring that bell.

Here I am now, 25 years later,

rapping about Jesus, no longer a hater, because of poor
choices, I fell into a crater, but He lifted me up, praise
God, my Creator.

I now have a testimony to save others from trouble, I
long for how God will use me outside this bubble, out
of the ashes, mire, and rubble,

the Lord has blessed my portion double.

I hope you enjoyed and got something out of this poem, Jeremy.
Always remember, Jesus Christ is real and the true hero of all time. He

is the one who laid down His life so we could live. With that being said, the best advice I or anyone else can give you is this: Believe in the Lord Jesus Christ and base your life upon the word of God.

Psalm 119:9 says, "Wherewithal shall a young man cleanse his way? By taking heed thereto according to thy word." In Ecclesiastes 12:13, Solomon breaks down life into its simplest form: "Fear God and keep His commandments, for this is the whole duty of man."

I personally have followed this advice, and because of it, my life is BLESSED. Recently, I received the greatest gift and blessing in my life besides my salvation. It was a direct result of being faithful and obedient to the word of GOD. Like Kurt Warner when he won the Super Bowl, I'm screaming, "THANK YOU JESUS!" for Kendra, Roselynn, Levi, Sampson and Jinx – my beautiful God-ordained wife, children and cats whom God brought into my life. They complete me and bless me with the honor of loving them, serving them, providing for them, and protecting them in true sheepdog fashion. THAT'S WHAT MY JESUS DOES! Jesus is the TRUTH, Jeremy. Believe that. Hallelujah.

God bless you, Jeremy. Look to Jesus and never give up. The only easy day was yesterday. I love you.

Philippians 2:9-11 and 4:13, Galatians 2:20

Jesus over everything.

ACCOMPLISHMENTS

- **Education:** M.A., Humanities (University of Houston-Clear Lake), B.S., Behavioral Science (University of Houston-Clear Lake), A.A., Liberal Arts (Alvin Community College), GED (Windham School District), Theology (More than Conquerors)
- **Programs/Certificates:** Voyager, House of Healing, Cognitive Intervention, Anger Management, Overcomers, Growing in Christ, Alpha, Bridges to Life, Marriage and Parenting, Financial Management, Quest for Authentic Manhood, Discovering Ethics, Contemplative Practice, Faith-Based Dorm (Mentor), hundreds of Bible correspondence certificates
- **Work/On-the-Job Training:** All-Around Presser, Alteration Tailor, Dryer, Warehouseman, Agriculture, Chaplain Support System Inmate, Education Support System Inmate, Unit Commissary, Unit Property, Warden Janitor's Squad, Kitchen (Line Server and Cook), Laundry (Folder, Janitor, Boot Room Clerk, Officer Clothing Clerk, Dryer, Presser, Sewer, Necessities Clerk, Stock Clerk)

13

GEORGE MARTIN RODRIGUEZ

My name is George Rodriguez, and I am serving life with parole plus 20 years, running concurrently. This journey started when I was 15 years old, around 25 years ago. Under current legislation, I won't be eligible for parole until 2024.

Dear George,

I wish I were there for you. Your upbringing and having your dad taken out of your life was not your fault. I know everybody believed he was guilty, but if you had someone to empathize with you instead of ignoring you, someone to believe with you in his innocence, then maybe you would not have distrusted authority–cops in particular. People's attitudes toward your father's incarceration were not against you.

I am sorry a broken heart misguided your understanding and you thought you had to trust other people instead of your family. Simply because you heard you were "like your father," the father that was hated and said to be a dog and guilty of a crime he did not commit, does not mean you are hated.

I know life was good prior to Dad going to prison. When he left and you felt alone, I noticed how you believed no one understood or cared. Yet, deep down in your heart, I know you knew Mama loved you. Otherwise, you would not have tried so hard to get her attention.

I felt your pain when at times you were blamed for something somebody else started. You have to understand that when Mama got mad at you, it was out of love. She wanted her boy to do right. Yet, as you grew into a teenager, you began to think older boys and men were the ones you should follow.

If you could, I would ask you to know your friends, because many of them are drug addicts and do not have a family. They have burned bridges. You have a family who cares for you! Family is valuable. Do not become blinded by the excitement of the streets or the feeling that you are accepted.

Now that you are in prison, and the loss of your son still hurts, do not push away the only woman who has stuck by your side. Mama will forever love you.

Yes, I know you feel you are going to die in prison and concerned that Mama will grow old and continue to visit you as you turn into a monster to survive. You might think she should forget you, but you are wrong! Do not listen to the lies of the devil; accept whatever consequences come for being your own man, but you were not a man.

You were a kid torn from a family and fed to wolves; embraced by the pack where you found acceptance and empathy. However, I imagine you lying awake at night, listening to the cries of others or sometimes your own as you reminisce being enticed by the smells of Mama's home-cooked meals or the donuts she stopped frying when she stopped smoking.

Those years have passed, and God has taken you out of a dark place. You can look in the mirror and know it is I who wishes I was there as the man I am now for the young boy you were. Nevertheless, my history has caused me/you to be more caring and understanding. Now you are the man Mama always wanted you to be. Continue on your journey in love.

Sincerely,

George Rodriguez

ACCOMPLISHMENTS

- **Education:** B.S. in Biblical Studies (Southwestern Baptist Theological Seminary), GED (Windham School District), Vocation in Auto Specialization (Air Conditioning and Heating)
- **Programs/Certificates:** Certificate of Service as a Lee College Tutor, Certified in Biblical Counseling (Southwestern Baptist Theological Seminary Walsh Counseling Center), OSHA General Industry Safety, Typing, Bridges to Life, Cognitive Intervention, Possum Talks, Malachi Dads, Family Forward, Quest, Making Peace with Your Past, The Quest for Authentic Manhood, Winning at Work and Home, What's So Amazing About Grace, Everybody's Normal until You Get to Know Them, Makarios (Supported by Sugar Creek Baptist Church), Kairos, The Man God Uses, Peer Health Educator, Mentorship in Faith-Based Community, Job Search Seminar, World Bible School Coursework, The Professional in Emergency Management (IS-513; Emergency Management Institute), Prisoners of Hope, Crossroads
- **Work/On-the-Job Training:** Butcher, Janitor, Stock Clerk, Waxing Floors, Landscaper, Gardener

14

MARGARET BATIZ

My name is Margaret Batiz. On January 26, 2008, I became a Second Looker. At the time of my incarceration, I was six months shy of my 17th birthday, awaiting the birth of my daughter who is now 11. On August 9, 2008, I was given a 50-year sentence for murder under the Law of Parties. Today I am 28. Today, my daughter Miesha is 11, and desperately awaiting my return home and back into society.

Dear Me,

You face a long journey, but be not weary, for this shall only make you stronger. It will seem that besides yourself you have no one, yet know, it is okay to trust and believe in others, because at times you will have to believe and trust in others to help carry you through. You will find these few diamonds in the rough who will be friends that you can count on who will share your pain as if it were their own. Believe in it, because you deserve it.

Listen to Mama, yeah, she seems to want to steal your fun days, but in your end days, you will realize the depth of that wisdom. Follow the paths that lead to potential and avoid the paths of merely well-trodden dirt which are fruitless. Set aside your dislike for school because one day your older self will feel inadequate and uneducated without it. You won't regret this! You're already confident and headstrong but stop thinking you know it all. You are only in your beginner's phase. Absorb it.

When you've experienced certain things and your belly produces life, make moments for the future of your child. She'll love you as if you've walked each milestone with her, and she'll know without a doubt she wasn't abandoned, so don't beat yourself up. You're not repeating the sins that you feel were your father's. Be strong. Look forward. Remember, you can't save the world.

One step at a time, but step with faith and belief because you'll need it. Head up. God's got you.

Margaret Batz

ACCOMPLISHMENTS

- **Programs/Certificates:** Voyager, Kairos Walk #36, Hope in the Storm
- **Work/On-the-Job Training:** Machine Operator, Laundry Press Operator

15

BRANDON BURNS BREWER

My name is Brandon Burns Brewer. At 16 years old I was sentenced to two consecutive sentences of 60 and 30 years in an adult maximum-security prison. I've currently been incarcerated for approximately 16 years, am now 32 years old, and will be eligible for parole under current legislation in 2034.

Dear Younger Me,

It's been approximately 16 years since we last talked. A lot has changed. I've now spent half your life in an adult, maximum-security prison. It hasn't been fun. Mom is dead, and Dad took his own life because he couldn't comprehend how he lost the love of his life to the other love of his life. And it seems as if your life is over; however, that's entirely up to the upcoming shots you're about to take.

I don't want to ask you any favors, but if you have the time, and from what I remember you have plenty, please ruminate over this. It's a second look from me to you.

I was asked to write one and I'm trying, I just, I want to give you a better shot at life.

See, the thing is: I know you want to be remembered. You want to leave a defining mark on the lives of others. But that all depends on the shots you take. Every moment is composed of a shot. And it's no one's shot but yours. Maybe you don't yet realize the impact your shots are having on those around you. But the world is so much bigger than it seems. I know you're more concerned with how many shots you take rather than concentrating on one memorable shot that will define how you'll be remembered. And isn't that what's causing you the most grief?

When Mom held a gun at Dad's forehead, I knew you were changing. But I didn't understand it. You asked Mom not to take the shot, all the while imagining how that one shot would put a stop to it all, to bring all the physical and verbal abuse to an end. You hardened yourself at that moment. You refused to cry, refused to show any emotion at all, but deep inside you were still an impressionable kid. Your dreams of becoming an NFL running back were still within grasp (yet dissolving right in front of your eyes), and I just wish I could have held you then, and willed you to imagine a world without your resolve to succeed, and what a worthless world that would be.

You're so young. Your entire life is laid out before you. Don't worry about how you're going to get from point A to point B because no matter what, you'll find a way there. You're a difference-maker, always have been, and from what I can tell, always will be. You're going to lead to see others succeed.

You have so much potential; hundreds, thousands, millions of people are counting on you. No matter where you end up in life, it's never too late. You may have missed opportunities, made some awful mistakes, been the harbinger of much pain and suffering into the lives of those you love, but in the grand scheme of things, you still have a shot to turn things around, to bring good into this world, to make a difference.

Younger me, we don't get to choose how many shots we have in this world, but we do have a say in making one shot count.

I'm not letting this one pass me by. I hope you won't either. Okay, Brandon Burns Brewer?

Sincerely,

ACCOMPLISHMENTS

- **Education:** M.Div. (Global University), B.S., Biblical Studies (Southwestern Baptist Theological Seminary), GED (Windham School District), Desktop Publishing College Trade (Alvin Community College), Certified Biblical Counselor (Southwestern Baptist Theological Seminary)
- **Programs/Certificates:** Epicenter Inside: Second Look Reentry Program (Program Developer and Facilitator), Reading is Freedom Literacy Program (Tutor), Making Peace with Your Past (Facilitator), Overcomers, Commitment to Change (Facilitator), Family Day Program (Program Developer), Voyager (Facilitator), Authentic Manhood, Faith-Based Dorm (Mentor, Program Developer, Facilitator), Job Skills and Reentry (Program Developer, Facilitator), Parole Forum (Program Developer, Facilitator), Experiencing God, Bridges to Life (Encourager and Facilitator), Cognitive Intervention Program, Toastmasters International (Phoenix Gavelier Club President, S.P.I.C.E. Gavelier Club President, Community of Orators Gavelier Club President), Certified Peer Health Educator
- **Work/On-the-Job Training:** Field Minister, College English Tutor (Southwestern Baptist Theological Seminary), Librarian Developer and Organizer (Southwestern Baptist Theological Seminary)
- **Other:** *Remember Me Bye* (novel releasing early 2020), "Life-Fulfilling Purpose" (*The UPPER ROOM* magazine), subject of a feature article (*Houston Chronicle* and *Austin American-Statesman*), "To Say Goodbye" (The Marshall Project)

16

MICHAEL ALAN TRACY

My name is Michael Alan Tracy. In 1994, at the age of 17, I was convicted of aggravated robbery (a crime in which nobody was injured, hurt, or killed) and sent to prison to serve a 60-year sentence. I am now 44 years old and have served 26 years of that sentence to date. Under current legislation, I will not be eligible for parole until I have served a minimum of half of my sentence (30 years), which will be in 2024.

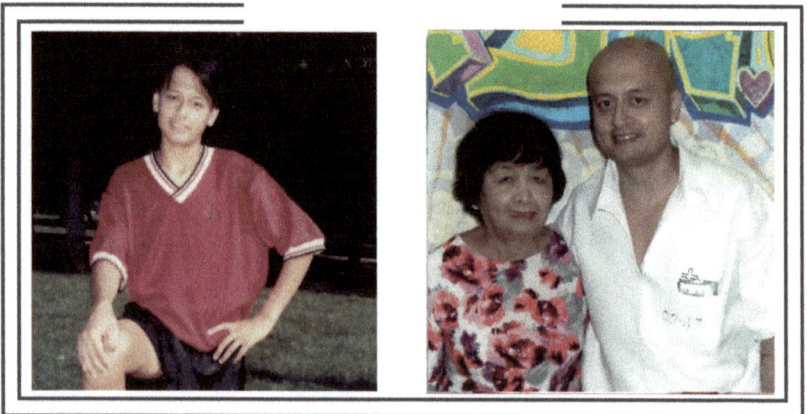

Dear Mikey,

I know you have high hopes, dreams, and aspirations in life, but you are currently adrift at sea with no sense of direction. You desire to follow in the footsteps of your dad, but you don't know how to do that. You possess the intellect and capacity to learn and excel in school, but you have problems with focus. You're in a season of trying to figure out who you are in all manners of life.

I'm sure you're asking at this point, "Who is this guy?" and "How does he know me so well?" The answer to both of these questions is: I am you.

You ask, "How is this possible?" I don't know how either, but the point is, I'm trying to stage an intervention in your life. All I can tell you is, that by God's grace I have been given this opportunity. Pay attention and listen carefully to what I am about to say. I should shout it because I pray that you take these things to heart before it's too late.

You are about to come to a moment in life where peer pressure is going to come to a head. You are going to be propositioned to participate in a crime by your "homeboys." One of them being your, so you think, "best friend." This is the apex in your life where you can go either way. These "friends" are going to ask you to participate more than five times. When this time comes, stand firm and say NO! This decision will decide if you're going to continue in life as a free man or come into prison for the next 26+ years of life. Yes, I have been locked up for 26 years, and am now 43 years old. I have lived all these years here wishing that at that moment I would have stood firm, spoken up for myself and not caved in to this peer pressure.

The main advice I have for you is to seek the face of God. What do I mean by that, you ask? I found out who Jesus Christ is while in prison, not while I was free. I had no idea who he was until I came to prison in 1994, and when I experienced him, I was in awe. But, immediately afterward, I made a mistake and allowed the devil to come in and entice me to participate in a way of life that was contrary to everything Mom and Dad taught me and what God desired for us – membership in a prison gang. I allowed that fire to go out for 18 years while I lived in sin and chased a lie, trying to become a legend inside the prison. And this same self-sabotaging way of thinking is the same mentality that will get you a life sentence if you don't watch out; that's what got me one!

I exhort you, I scream at you, to wake up while you have the chance. Stop putting celebrities, rappers, thugs, and gang members on a pedestal. Stop allowing yourself to be influenced by people who say they are your "friends." The day after you get locked up, they will just be looking for the next idiot to fill your shoes.

Sincerely,

ACCOMPLISHMENTS

- **Education:** GED (Windham School District)
- **Programs/Certificates:** Redemption Workshop, Honor Thy Father + Mother, Quest for Authentic Manhood, Bridges to Life (Encourager), College Seminary Classes (Fight the Good Fight of Faith, Bible Interpretation, Making Him L.O.R.D., Conversion and Calling, The Kingdom of God, Spiritual Warfare), The Christian Life (Bible Study), Freedom Weekend, Life Recovery, Overcomers
- **Work/On-the-Job Training:** Drying Machine Operator, Washing Machine Operator, Clothing Presser Operator, Stock Clerk, General Clerk, Assistant to the Chaplain
- **Other:** Christian Baptism

17

SHERRARD OWENS WILLIAMS

My name is Sherrard Owens Williams and I was born and raised in San Antonio Texas. On October 18, 1994, at the age of 15, I was certified as an adult to stand trial. In 1995, I was convicted under the Law of Parties for Capital murder and given a mandatory and automatic life sentence. I am now 41 years old and have been incarcerated for 26 years. I must serve 40 calendar years under current legislation before becoming eligible for parole consideration at age 55 in 2034.

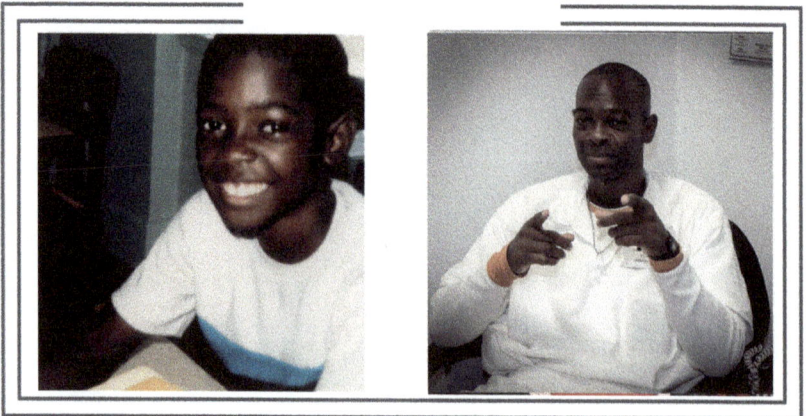

Dear Young Sherrard,

On July 22, 1994, I entered not only another cold world but also a cold environment within the Texas penal system. I was only able to breathe for a short period of 15 years through a respiratory system of freedom in society. I was being processed through the three phases of juvenile, county jail, and finally multiple prison facilities. Although this allowed me to face some demons of my past and begin a shift in thinking from a naive adolescent to a mature man, I desperately want to save you from this trouble.

There is another way. Turn to God and make a 180 with your life. If not, this reality will soon be yours too. Take heed of my experiences and save yourself from destruction. Lean on the Lord and He will make your path straight.

My initiation to prison occurred upon my arrival at the Terrell Unit (now Polunsky) in 1996. It was heralded by inmates as the "Terrell Dome" and at times called, "A Rocking and Rollin' Terrell Dome" by officers. I began to grasp the fact that everything and everyone around me was serious. I was forced to embrace uncertainties for survival.

Throughout my years in the Terrell Unit, I had countless fights. One event consisted of being attacked with a hand-fashioned shank (made from a metal trash can handle) and assaulting an inmate with a metal trash can. I started to give up on everything and lost hope.

In 2002, I was assigned to administrative segregation. This caused me to become deeply introspective and question my life direction. I reflected on all the wrongs I did as a child and all the ways I felt wronged by others. I asked God why he took people I loved out of my life and out of this world.

Why did He make my childhood so difficult for me to understand and embrace?

Why did He allow me to survive being shot in the stomach, a car wreck from a high-speed chase (95-100 mph), and a host of other senseless gang-related events?

Was this His divine punishment for all I had done wrong in my childhood?

God's message to me was clear, "Stop doing wrong, my son."

I had harbored significant rage, resentment, and bitterness within me, so I asked God to forgive me and help with forgiving others. I began to detox emotionally, replacing negative for positive, evil for peace, a broken vessel for a fixed vessel, an empty vessel for a filled vessel. My mind as a youngster began to renew and transformation ensued. I pleaded with God to shape me into a son He would be proud to claim.

In 2005, I was released from administrative segregation and my journey to "stop doing wrong" had begun. In 2007, after a two-year investigation, I was offered the chance to complete and sign my Gang Renouncement and Disassociation (GRAD) paperwork. It changed my life and as a result, I have helped others change their lives from gang relations.

Since breaking free from the bondage of my previous life, I have embraced spiritual renewal and am learning to become a new man – one who is affable, competent, focused, and a new creation who is driven by a purpose to "stop doing wrong." It's an honor to teach others to do the same.

The Bible says, "Better is the end of a thing than the beginning thereof." (Eccl. 7:8) This scripture truly ignites my spirit.

Although I started in a losing battle, I have become the man God says I am because of Christ in me. He has given me a divine purpose and rewarded me with an eternal home with Him.

Christ's Love,

Sherrard Williams

ACCOMPLISHMENTS

- **Education:** GED (Windham School District), Vocational Trade of Construction Fundamentals: Core Curriculum
- **Programs/Certificates:** Introductory Craft Skills, Construction Site Safety Orientation, OSHA 10 Construction Safety, Financially Literacy Certificate (Acceleron Learning), Peer Health Education Course Certificate, Texas Department of Criminal Justice Safe Prison Program Sexual Assault Awareness Certificate, Peer Health Education Training (HIV / AIDS Education and Prevention Conference Course), Peer Health Conference (Walk Talk Education and Prevention Conference Certificate), Toastmaster Public Speaking Certificate, Bridges to Life, Kairos Walk #32, Voyager, Authentic Manhood, Biblical Interpretation, 2020 Eighteenth Annual Peer Education Health Conference Certificate
- **Work:** Warehouseman, Administrative General Clerk (Chapel of Hope), Administrative Education Department Janitor, Janitor, Laundry Department, Industrial Truck Operator (Forklift), Main Kitchen Department, General Library Clerk, Maintenance General Clerk, General Clerk of Chapel, Epicenter Advisory Board, Epicenter Unit Leader

18

STEPHANIE BARRON

M y name is Stephanie Barron, I am 37 years old and was a naive and impressionable 17-year-old when I got locked up in 1999. In October of 2000, I received two 75-year sentences to run concurrently. I will be eligible for parole in 2029.

Dear Stephanie,

I wish that I could go back and change so many things, starting with reassuring you that Mom and Dad love you dearly. The most important people in your life are your family members. You should cherish the time you have with them. You were so spoiled and self-centered, thinking that you knew everything, yet you didn't have a clue.

You should have stayed in school and not worried so much about what your boyfriend was doing. As 1 Corinthians 15:33 states – "BAD associations spoil useful habits." That wasn't love – real love comes from your family, and it takes time and boundaries to establish healthy relationships.

There are days I still don't fully understand how you allowed yourself to get so completely lost and off track. All that can be done now is to be the woman I know that Mom and Dad would want me to be despite the environment of where I am today.

I'm glad you never got involved in drugs. I sit here at times, thanking God for things He may have saved me from, for example, the road that you were on with your relationship. Who knows where I would've ended up otherwise. I try not to dwell on the "what ifs" of yesterday but instead push forward to have a better future.

You had the perfect childhood and should have been more appreciative rather than taking everything for granted. You allowed one boy to control your thoughts, and that's not what a relationship is supposed to be about. You should have been worried about graduating from high school and pursuing the career you wanted as an elementary school teacher. You will regret bad decisions for the rest of your life.

Truly,

Stephanie Barron

ACCOMPLISHMENTS

- **Education:** Enrolled in college to pursue an associate degree
- **Programs/Certificates:** Bridges to Life
- **Work/On-the-Job Training:** Landscaper, Plumber, Painter, Carpenter, Floor Waxer, Gardener

19

HENRY WESLEY MOLINA, JR.

M y name is Henry Wesley Molina, Jr. I became incarcerated while in high school at the age of 17, in 1998. I am 39, and have been incarcerated for 22 years. As things stand now, I will not be eligible for parole until 2028, when I am 47 years old.

Hey, Wesley,

It's me...or rather, it's you, 22 years later. The year is 2020! Hard to believe, right? I already know what you're doing. You want to throw this to the side, think it's a joke, but please just read it. You'll still make it to wherever you're planning to go.

This isn't a joke. It's a rare opportunity to receive insight. Remember the show you liked, *Quantum Leap*, where one could go back in time and change history? Well, I didn't make it through the portal, but this letter did!

Your mom and dad love you. They want what is best for you. They see you throwing away your life. Your mom stays up all night in the living room waiting for you to come home. She dozes off here and there, sitting up, praying you make it home, and she still has to go to work the next day. She can't sleep next to her husband (your dad) because she is restless, and her oldest child isn't home. Although it makes you feel bad, it doesn't change you. Next time you walk in and she comes to you with red eyes from crying and lack of sleep, and hugs you, know this: You're breaking her heart, but still she loves you! Because you didn't change, one day you never made it back home. Your family was never the same. Mom needed you!

Your dad works hard to create and establish a company for you and your siblings to run one day. I know your dream is to play on the same softball team as him and dress in jeans and boots like him. Oh yeah! Now do you believe this is your writing, for who else could know that? He loves you. He's hard on you, but you know he loves you. He is the greatest man that you'll ever know. Listen to him. Enjoy your friendship with him.

Know this: Because you didn't change, you never got to play on his team or work for him. Both of your dreams never happened. It broke his heart more than yours! Dad needed you too!

Your little brother looks up to you, but you show him wrong. I know he is your road dog and best friend, but you need to show him right.

Know this: The day you never came home, he was never the same. He made straight A's, but he was so hurt that he never even finished high school. He needed you too!

Your baby sister. Yeah, I see you smiling! She is your little princess. She adores you. Remember picking her up from daycare when she introduced you to her entire class? She grows up without you because you didn't listen. She needed you too!

Don't go live in Carriage Lane! Go home to your family before curfew. Stop skipping classes. Do your work. Start going to church again. Help those in need.

I know you're not a bad kid, but you'll make one mistake in your life and change your and your family's lives forever. You are found guilty of murder and sentenced to 60 years in prison. But more than that, you also cause pain and hurt to another human being and his family. They too suffered, and it will hurt you more than you can imagine.

One night, you'll get a flat tire where you are the only guy in a car with nine girls. Oh yes! You are so lucky! You'll fix the flat tire and get all of them home safely, but a girl named Ashley will be in the front seat. Yes, I know you know who she is. Tell her what you're feeling and show her this letter. She needed you too! But still, get her home safely. She'll become your wife and bless you with three handsome sons. Yes, you are so lucky, but you were only blessed like this because you changed your life and surrendered yourself to Jesus!

This is who I am now (who you are now), the one writing this letter. I am writing this to you, my younger self, to open your eyes, so you can change now, in 1998, and not wait until later. I'm trying to save others the pain you caused them, and yourself; a mom having to bury her son. Your parents, brother, sister, and later, wife and kids visit you in prison. Ten solid years of solitary confinement, and so far, 22 years of loneliness and hell.

Do what is right. Stay away from evil. Don't let your so-called "friends" mislead you. Stay away from drugs. Cry out for help when you need it. Love one another and be a beacon of light to those lost.

My younger self, you needed me, the way I am now. I am sorry I didn't see it then. But oh, I do now! Wesley, you needed you too!

Be The Best You,

Henry Molina

ACCOMPLISHMENTS

- **Education:** GED (Windham School District), A.A.S., Business Management & Administration (Lee College)
- **Programs/Certificates:** Certificates in Diesel Mechanics, Entrepreneurship, International Business, Marketing, Supervision, Management, and Business (Lee College), OSHA General Industry Safety Certificate, Authentic Manhood, Men's Fraternity, Faith 101, Kairos Walk #4, Cognitive Intervention, Anger Management, Substance Abuse Classes, and Gang Renouncement and Disassociation, Bridges to Life (currently enrolled)
- **Work/On-the-Job Training:** Peer Tutor (Lee College), Library Assistant (Windham School District), Peer Tutor (Windham School District)
- **Other:** Alpha Beta Gamma Business Honor Society

20

TAMIKA NICOLE WHALEY BENJAMIN

L ooking in the mirror perplexed and bewildered, I think, who am I? I'm Tamika Nicole Whaley Benjamin. In 1997, I was 16 years old and sentenced to life in prison. I've been incarcerated for 23 years. I am now 40 years old, and under current legislation won't be eligible for parole until 2035.

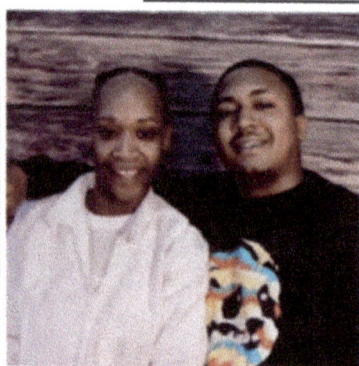

Dear Tamika,

By the time you read this letter, my prayers are you've opened your eyes and matured into your own woman. You were just a teenager when you found out you were given away by your biological mother to be raised by your stepmother. This wasn't because of anything you did – instead, look at it as if you're being saved!

You hid your feelings but acted out through your emotions. You were confused about wanting a relationship with your birth mother and not appreciating the stern love and responsibilities shown to you by your stepmother. You became rebellious, kept running away, hanging with the wrong crowd, knowing you should've been listening to Mama, a lot of opportunities passed you by as you gave up on running track in junior high, neglecting chores and church services. You had so many talents – singing, dancing – but babysitting was your favorite.

Throughout your struggles, Mama tried to tell you right from wrong. By age 14 you discovered boys – one, in particular, was a "bad boy." That's when you spiraled out of control. You lost all innocence allowing him to control you and abuse you verbally and physically.

You quickly became someone else. Disrespecting your mother, you started staying out all night drinking, smoking weed, and selling crack. Your style of dress was different, but of course, Mama never turned her back on you. She even accepted you being with this "bad boy" because of seeing how adamant you were about him. She kept praying and hoping you would change. A mother's prayer is unconditional.

At age 15, you were allowed to get married, which was definitely your biggest mistake. You put your trust in him, gave him your all, you were so naive, manipulated and blinded by what you thought was love. Never live life on someone else's terms. His jealousy rants were getting out of control.

One night, he came home and startled you out of your sleep to come and go with him. You went, not wanting to argue or fight with him. You walked right into a trap where three older guys (him included) had planned to rob a motel. You were used as bait and now you're here with a life sentence for capital murder.

Know your self-worth. Love yourself and live life on your own terms.

Sincerely,

Tamika Benjamin

ACCOMPLISHMENTS

- **Education:** GED (Windham School District)
- **Programs/Certificates:** Captivating Experience, Certificate of Hard Work, History of Religion, College Business, Hope in the Storm
- **Work/On-the-Job Training:** Plumbing, Carpentry, Stock Clerk, Drying Operations, Cooking

21

DAVID MCMILLAN

My name is David McMillan. I have been incarcerated since my arrest in Smith County in December of 1993. At the age of 17, I received two concurrent life sentences and I am currently 43 years old. I am eligible for parole in 2023. In the 26 years since my incarceration began, I have achieved much growth, maturity, and rehabilitation as well as many certificates for various programs and educational studies.

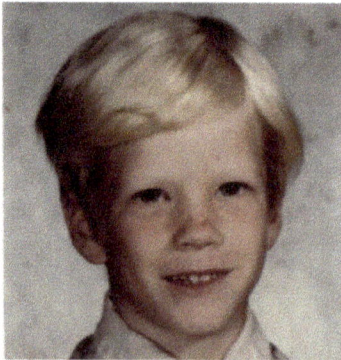

David,

This letter may seem strange at first, but by the end, it will all make sense. Let me start by saying: Mom and Dad are right. What people say about you doesn't matter. What you believe about yourself is most important.

You are going to make bad grades and fail classes, but this doesn't mean you are stupid or slow, as some people will tell you. You just learn differently. When you finally teach yourself how to learn, because everyone else has given up on you, your appetite for learning will become insatiable. This is very important. Whatever else you do in life, DO NOT drop out of high school. If you do, it will set in motion a series of events that will cost you so much that, at times, death will seem like a better deal.

You are going to fall in love and have your heart broken a couple of times before you turn 18. You are going to lose yourself in who others think you are or what they think you should be. You will see that everyone who claims to be your friend abandons you once it is not convenient for them. The ones you have betrayed and hurt the most are going to anchor you when they want to fall apart themselves. These are the people that will sacrifice for you. You are going to act like you know what it means to be a man but no one will see the confused child you are on the inside.

You need to believe in yourself. Quit saying, "I can't" because of your fear of being a failure. Instead, you need to say, "I'll try." It is okay to fail, it just shows you a way that doesn't work. Mom and Dad love you, even if they don't say it or at times don't show it. They just know how to love as they were taught. It will get to the point where every time y'all talk, "I love you" will be said and meant.

You have a Bible you will never read. The Story of it will never be explained to you, or even told to you. Pull that Bible out and read it. You need to take its Story to heart, learn the morals of the men who followed Christ, and become like them. Apply the teachings of Christ to your young life and know that your affirmation of manhood comes from God alone. Only then will you truly be free to be the man you are called to be. You are free from everything that says you're not a man.

A wise man once said, "I have often thought about what I would say to my younger self if I could. How could I talk sense into him, to keep him from making the same decisions I did and ruining his life and the lives of others the way I did. But, I can't; he is gone and all that is left is this tired old man."

That was very powerful to me because he said it while sitting before the parole board after serving a life sentence. I write this to you, my younger self, while sitting in prison, serving a life sentence, as a tired old man waiting on parole.

So I ask you, please, for us, live your life differently.

ACCOMPLISHMENTS

- **Education:** GED (Tyler Independent School District)
- **Programs/Certificates:** Christian Life, Ferguson Mental Health Stress Management (Certificate of Achievement), Cognitive Intervention Program (Certificate of Achievement), Bible Study in Christian Growth, Peer Health Education Course, Voyager, Purpose Driven Life, Overcomers, The Urban Ministry Institute (Fight the Good Fight of Faith, Making Him Lord, Conversion and Calling, Kingdom of God, Foundations of Christian Leadership, Evangelism & Spiritual Warfare, Bible Interpretation), Successful Completion of Transformation III, Freedom Weekend (Spiritual Encounter with God; Refined by Fire: From Pain to Purpose), Life Recovery, The Bible in 90 Days, Bridges to Life (Participant and Encourager), Quest for Authentic Manhood, Taking Anger Seriously, Steppin' Out, Kairos, Faith-Based Dorm
- **Work/On-the-Job Training:** Warehouseman, Material Coordinator, General Clerk, Computer Operator

22

REAZ AHMED

M y name is Reaz Ahmed. I was given an 85-year sentence at age 16. Over the past 24 years, I have worked diligently to prepare myself for the day when I can be given a second look, God willing.

Dear Reaz,

It has been a long time since we last met. Well, 24 years to be exact. Yet, I still remember everything about you as if I never left you. Your spirit, energy, and thoughts reside within my being. I believe if we were to meet today, we would have a lot to share. I'm positive that your curiosity would overwhelm me with questions. Although I may not possess all the answers, I would certainly counsel you with words of wisdom, knowledge, and understanding.

The main theme I want to cover is CHOICES. Each choice you make impacts both you and others. One devastating choice determined many of my life experiences to date. In hindsight, I completely understand how it inflicted pain and suffering on others, causing me to lose my identity, family, and lifestyle. Therefore, I believe it is my moral responsibility to help you understand how even the smallest choice can have a devastating and life-changing domino effect.

I know there is an awkward feeling you struggle to understand about yourself. You continue to sense that a negative event is going to take place within your teenage years. Although you are unable to pinpoint the origin of that feeling, it is a thought that does not leave you. I strongly suggest you seek counseling in regard to those thoughts. By speaking with someone, you will be on a path toward exploring your thoughts and finding yourself.

I know it is not easy for you to share your feelings with others. However, it is the only method that will help your psychological wellness. As you learn how your mind operates, you will understand why you think, function and act the way you do. This lesson will be crucial to your development because it will teach you to focus on your strengths and weaknesses.

There are many characteristics you will learn to develop. However, only two in particular demand your focus: PRIDE and SHAME. Both of these traits will have positive and negative effects on your life. For me, these traits played a lead role in causing my negative actions, which destroyed two separate families.

Your destiny doesn't have to be the same as mine. I know you come from a good family and were raised with godly morals and values.

I remember you being a prideful person. You refuse to let ANYONE make you feel like you need them. The truth is you do. No one can make it in life completely alone. Regardless of how mentally strong you are, you seem to make irrational decisions when it comes to your pride. Believe me, it takes a strong man to realize his weakness. Learn how to put your pride aside and rationally deal with your emotions. Become a man of integrity because that should be the compass for your daily choices.

I believe God placed shame in our hearts to help keep us consciously pure. We all have an internal gauge to distinguish between right and wrong. When we commit a wrongful act, we experience shame and also fear the judgment it brings without contemplating the punishment. The fear of shame is the greatest issue you need to address, because it can cause you to plunge into further darkness.

At some point in your life, you might put yourself in a shameful position. In that moment, think about the consequences for your action before you react. Your ability to respond to shame will be a key indicator for setting your path to the future.

In closing, the most important message for you is this: your thoughts will shape your character, your character will determine your actions, and your actions will ultimately build your life. I pray that you receive my message with an open heart and transform into the man we both know you can become.

Stay focused.

ACCCOMPLISHMENTS

- **Education:** M.A., Humanities (University of Houston-Clear Lake), B.S., Behavioral Science (University of Houston-Clear Lake), A.A., General Liberal Arts (Alvin Community College), GED (Windham School District), College Vocational Trade in Computer Repair and Computer Science (Alvin Community College)

- **Programs/Certificates:** Youthful Offender Program, Cognitive Intervention, Peer Health and Sexual Assault Awareness, Bridges to Life (Peer Facilitator), Voyager, Authentic Manhood I & II, Marriage and Parenting, Possum Talks, Faith- Based Dorm, Safe Prisons Seminar, Parole Packet Workshop, Lee College Debate Team, Tutor (Lee College), First Contact Reentry Program, Peer Education Coordinator, Unit Peer Educator, Parole Packet Workshop (Facilitator), Faith-Based Dorm (Family Leader; Community Care Coordinator; Teacher), Iron Man Health and Wellness Awareness, Lifer's Lifestyle Public Speaking Class (Coordinator), Toastmasters

- **Work/On-the-Job Training:** All-Around Welder, Forklift Safety and Operations, OSHA General Industry Safety, General Office Clerk, Stock Control Clerk, Warehouseman, All-Around Presser, Washing Machine Operator, Stock Control Clerk (Laundry), Agriculture, Janitor (Living Area), Clothing Exchanger (Laundry), Inside Landscaper, Janitor (Education Department), Stock Control Clerk (Laundry), Office Clerk (Laundry), Kitchen Helper (Lineman; Vegetable Prep; Linebacker; First-Shift Cook), All-Around Painter (Laundry), Office Clerk (Kitchen), Inside Compound, Upholstery (Furniture Factory), General Clerk (Mechanical), Unit Artist, Woodworker, Artist, Metal Worker (Craft Shop)

23

VICTORIA S. HARRIS

M y name is Victoria Harris and I was 17 years old when the unspeakable happened in 2004. I was given a capital life sentence and have done 16 years. I am 33 years old and won't be eligible for parole until 2045.

Dear Victoria,

Where do I start? I want so badly to save you from the painful memories I carry around in my mind. My heart aches to show you that there was a better way to handle your shame, guilt and the need to feel a love that only God could give you. The love you craved and chased was with you all along but you didn't know it yet.

Do you remember all the long talks you shared with your parents? Dad said you needed to get your education. He's right, Victoria, because, without it, doors are harder to open. Please listen and get your education. Don't listen to those family members when they tell you "you'll never amount to anything" because you can do all things through Christ who strengthens you.

Love yourself and know your worth. People will only do to you what you allow them to do, so have values and boundaries. Oh, how you need to set boundaries to your love because you love hard, deep, and that's all very important to you. However, it must be a healthy love with healthy boundaries. Don't allow it to consume you to the point of losing yourself in other people's wants and desires. Look around you and see life's value. You are so much smarter than you give yourself credit for. Remember the morals and values you were taught and don't settle for anything less than you know you deserve. Learn that life is not all about you.

If only you looked around you, it would be clear there are others hurting as well. Those tears your parents shed were due to your lack of communication and the result of you wanting your way. But you have NO clue what your own way is. I understand you feel alone and think no one understands you, but you must take the risk and speak up so wrongs can be corrected and addressed. Learn to trust your mother because she loves you and doesn't understand when you push her away. You will come to learn that family is all you have. Tuck them under your arms and don't be self-centered. They are hurting too.

Know that your actions will always affect someone else. Hurt people hurt people, so learn to work through your hurt. Be a kid, Victoria; don't try and grow up too fast. Your parents only want to protect you and give you a better life. Everything you are trying to be for your significant other you need to stop and learn to be those things for yourself. You can't truly love someone if you can't first love God and yourself. The blind and lost can't lead each other. Don't take the small things in life for granted. Hold your head up and keep moving forward.

Love your older self,

Victoria Harris

ACCOMPLISHMENTS

- **Education:** GED (Windham School District)
- **Programs/Certificates:** Purpose Driven Life, Cognitive Intervention, Kairos, Truth Be Told (Pay it Forward), Faith-Based Dorm, Patriot Paws
- **Work/On-the-Job Training:** Counter Attendant, Pressing Officers' Uniforms, Washing Machine Operator, General Clerk

24

JENNIFER JEFFLEY

My name is Jennifer Jeffley, and I am serving a capital life sentence with parole eligibility after 40 calendar years. At the time of my incarceration, I was 56 days into my 15th birthday. 23 years later, I am now 38. If I am required by current law to serve the full 40 years before parole consideration, I have a mandated 17 years left to serve, upon which time I will be 55 years of age.

Dear Jennifer,

In time you will realize you're worthy and strong beyond measure. Be unafraid. Your true self is your best self. Loyalty doesn't cost a thing, nor will it put you in harm's way. Trust your mom and believe, because despite it all she will never leave you to face the world alone. Enjoy your youth because you're only young once. Be proud of your individualism and embrace it, for trends, popularity, and fads come and go. Hold to your nature. It's okay to say "no" when your conscience is arguing with your impetuous decision.

Lead by example and not by the desire to fit in and be accepted. Your love for self should always be enough. There will be times when you feel alone and misunderstood, but those are the aches of growing pains.it won't always be this dark. Know this too and believe it with all your heart: If you had kept Tomas home even a few minutes longer, it wouldn't have kept him safe. You're too young to carry guilt because you're too young to fully understand responsibility. It wasn't your fault. It's okay to hurt – express it, the weight of the world doesn't belong to a child. Stay honest because the integrity of your word is all you shall have.

Again, don't be afraid. You will face many dark times in your life but faith shall always light your path. At the end of all this, you'll be a woman created of all the small things oft-forgotten and molded from all the big things once denied. You will rise higher and impact lives in a way you never imagined. Be brave and stay true to yourself. It's okay to be different and say "no." Mama will never give up on you.

You will go far and achieve much, but this will be one of the harshest lessons in your life. Do NOT be discouraged nor deterred. You will touch lives and break hearts, but those broken shards will penetrate customs and help break the mold. You are a fighter! With this passion, never stop fighting for what you believe in most and to be heard.

There will be times you are turned away and other times when people won't believe you. In these moments give everything to God and let Him leave His footprints in your sands. Stay encouraged and always believe. Your belief only needs to be the size of mustard seed.

Give thanks, even in your times of despair, and always, always, keep God first. He hears you even when you believe your calling card has expired. There is never an expiration, He hears you, so listen. Head up, eyes dry, faith strong, and march, soldier. March. Your battle won't last a lifetime. Good luck, little one, and know you're loved. Tremendously and unconditionally.

Lovingly,

Jennifer Jefflal

ACCOMPLISHMENTS

- **Education:** GED (Windham School District) as TDCJ's Youngest Female Graduate, A.A., General Studies, A.A., Business Management (Central Texas College)
- **Programs/Certificates:** Sisters Taking a New Direction (Co-Founder), Cook's Apprenticeship Class, Braille Program, Breaking Free (Certificate Designer), Various Bible Classes
- **Work/On-the-Job Training:** Landscaper, Cook, Laundry Machine Operator, All-Around Press Operator, Janitor, Cylinder Press Operator, Offset Press, Chemical Distributor, Floor Crew, Paint Squad, Bootblack

25

JUSTIN IAN DUDIK

My name is Justin Dudik. I am more than just a TDCJ number. I was 15 years old when I was incarcerated in 1993. I was sentenced to 99 years, of which I have done 26 calendar years flat on so far. I am 42 years old now and will be eligible for parole in 2024.

Hey, guess who? It's me.

It's you!

You will never believe where you are, but no matter what, it's better than where you were headed. Before you get here, I want to talk to you about some things you think you already know. You think you have it all figured out, but let me tell you, you don't! The things you think are important are not. The most important things are right in front of you.

You will come to realize the value of things you can't touch. Character, principles, respect, loving those who love you even more than you love yourself. These are some of the greatest assets that will last your whole life – longer than any material possessions – but you will have to lose everything to appreciate this.

I look at pictures of you and wish you could see the kid that everyone else sees. You are not grown! Your fear of failure and judgment turn you into a kid looking for approval and acceptance. You are so good at it almost nobody notices, but I do. I know you better than anybody. I am you.

You have to slow down and appreciate your experiences. Remember as much as you can about how you were feeling in those moments because for a long period of your life, memories will be all you have. Memories to live life, memories to be with the ones you love, memories of what everyone else was doing while you are doing what I am doing.

It will hurt when you start to forget the last time you slept under a roof with your family, celebrated anything with the ones who pray for you to succeed, or were disciplined by someone whose authority is more deserving. Forgetting the last time you were embraced by one of your loved ones without having to say goodbye will be hardest.

It hurts when life has to move on even though you wish you could slow it down and put it all into perspective. Be thankful for all the things you have. Everything has unique value, don't always want more. Your parents want you to mature at a natural pace. I know you think everything your parents tell you is a challenge you have to win. Trust me, it's not. When you are older you will understand the unconditional love your mom and dad have for you!

You don't realize it, but your dad is everything you wish you were as a man. Watch and listen to him more closely. He is an amazing man who, even from a distance, instills some of your best qualities in you. Life is about emulating the positive role models around you. Your mom was your best friend then and still is today. You will be amazed by her strength. It still takes my breath away knowing her strength carried me through all my fears of the unknown. Do more as a son, but know it will never be enough to equal what your parents will do for you.

Your brother and sister should be your friends. You should enjoy their company and also appreciate the loyalty that comes with being blood. All the things you do affect your whole household, and even though you are a kid, you are the guilty one.

I have to tell you about where I am before you get here. You should be scared! Imagine being in the midst of thousands of people and feeling you are alone, but never being able to show it. Everyone is watching and waiting to exploit your emotions. You wanted to be a man, but even though you are not, they treat you like one or less. They view you as a kid thrown into hell here on earth. The things you see, hear and do are only part of your nightmares while you sleep right now. When you are here you will realize you are awake and the nightmares are real.

It's hard, you're alone, you're scared. I know, remember I'm you.

The people in your life now don't always have your best interest in mind. It's no longer unconditional because everything has a price. You wonder what path led you here, but when you turn around, the path back is no longer there and where you are going is nowhere in sight. Take a look around and say goodbye because it's almost time. Soak it all in because I don't know when you will make it back.

The smallest details matter because everything is going to change! I can tell you, you don't want to be me, but I would give anything to be you again. Unfortunately, I will see you soon. Until then, know I love you and I'm here waiting for you.

Justin

ACCOMPLISHMENTS

- **Education:** B.A., Humanities (In Progress; University of Houston), A.A. Arts (Trinity Valley Community College), GED, Barber College, Correspondence Courses at Louisiana State University
- **Programs/Certificates:** GED Tutor, Anger Management, Alcoholics Anonymous, Cognitive Intervention Classes, Marriage and Parenting, Toastmasters, Prison for a Day (Member)

26

DELVIN ROSHON MOUTON

H ello! My name is Delvin Roshon Mouton. I was born in Houston, Texas in 1978. At the age of 15, I was arrested for capital murder. (My first ever offense.) I was certified as an adult and given a capital life sentence. I am currently required to serve a minimum of 40 calendar years before being eligible for the chance of parole. At the time of this writing, I am 41 years old and entering my 26th year of incarceration. I won't be eligible for parole for 15 years.

To my younger self,

Wow! If you only knew. I want to tell you first of all that Mom and Dad, yes, they love you more than you may ever know. Everything they tried to tell you was only for your good. All the talks, all the butt whipping; yes, brother, they were truly for your good. I know Dad was hard at times, but he had to be. Why? Because life is not easy. Every choice, every decision you make will not only affect you, but everyone connected to you.

All those times you were made to set out early in the morning to cut the yard, wash the cars, do the dishes, clean your room; it was all to make you into a responsible, disciplined and humble man someday. No, they were not mean when they warned you about certain people and going to certain places. They were only trying to help you avoid some of the pitfalls of life. Dad tried to teach you through you pulling weeds from the flower beds. Why? Because bad company corrupts good morals!

Hey. I know you get tired of Pop and Grandma always taking you to church and always putting God into everything. Well, they know what they are talking about as well! My advice is that you take advantage of the foundation they are trying to lay for you. You are their first grandchild. They believe in you. They want God's best for you. They see the potential, they see who you can be! Delvin, listen, pay attention. They both are full of wisdom. You will need lots of wisdom to make it in this life. You will constantly hear Pop say, "Preach all the time. Use words when you have to!" You'll get that later. Trust me. I did! You will always have a sphere of influence. Others will look to you for guidance, for leadership. Again, every decision counts.

Listen, I know you want to be like your uncles and have this girl and that girl. Yeah, it sounds good! But that is not the way to go. Save yourself for that one special lady. It's worth it. Don't just give yourself to anyone and everyone. You are putting yourself at risk. You are exposing yourself to things you can't fathom right now. Save yourself. Wait! Don't let those around you decide your future for you. Just because they jump off the cliff doesn't mean you have to follow. Be your own person. Set the standard and do not lower it. And by the way, having a bunch of money, clothes, etc., is all overrated. In the end, none of that matters. Your character matters. You making quality decisions matter. Your faith matters. Your friends can't live your life for you. You must live it yourself. None of them are here with me now.

Oh yeah, what is "now"? 41 years old in prison! No prom, no college scholarships, no car, not even a driver's license! No job, no income, no social security. Things that matter later in life. See, allowing your friends to decide for you caused you to try a life of crime. Your first time touching a gun causes you to destroy another family and your future in the process. How? Because you thought you knew it all! I found out, you don't! Yes, Mom and Dad are still supporting you, loving you, and sacrificing for you. Grandma is just trying to hold on. Pop, well he passed on over. Your brothers and sisters (yeah you will have two brothers and three sisters), they look up to you. Remember, all of your choices matter! All those girls you try to impress by doing things you were not raised to do; none of them are here now. Think about that!

Delvin, don't lose your life trying to be someone you were not called to be. You have a great future ahead of you. Even with some of the mistakes of life, you have a great life ahead. You have been called to be a great influence in the Lord. You will be an amazing husband and father too! You are going to go on to preach and sing the gospel of Jesus Christ! You are going to author books, teach generations and change the world. Your life has a purpose, it has meaning! Stay focused. Stay the course. There are great days ahead. But you must make quality decisions now! I could go on and on but the paper may run out. Love yourself. Listen to those who have come before you and let God be God in your life. I pray that you take heed to these words because they will save you at least 25 years of incarceration!

Love you,

P.S. Let me pray with you:

Heavenly Father,

I thank you for this chance to spend time with the younger version of Delvin. I am humbled by this experience. Father, I just ask that even as he makes mistakes and decisions that may lead him away from you, protect him O God! Put people in his life that will not give up on him, People that will love him for the man you will grow him to be! Draw him close to you in all he goes through. Give him wisdom, knowledge, and understanding! Overwhelm him with your love; overtake him with your truth and overflow his life with your grace and mercy! This is my prayer in the mighty majestic, marvelous, matchless name of Jesus Christ!

Amen!

ACCOMPLISHMENTS

- **Education:** GED (Windham School District)
- **Programs/Certificates:** Computer Repair, Culinary Arts, Faith-Based Program (Worship and Leadership Class Leader, Facilitator for 64 Programs), Christian Living Bible study, Administrative Segregation Minister, Certified Peer Educator, Certificate of Ordination, Texas A&M Agrilife Extension Program
- **Work/On-the-Job Training:** Cook, Butcher, Baker
- **Other:** Published author of *What God Told Me* (Christian Faith Publishing)

27
___

ANTHONY MAURICE LEWIS

M y name is Anthony Lewis. Because of a series of bad choices I made as a 16-year-old on February 18, 1997, I have spent the past 23 years in prison. I am now 39, but based on current legislation won't be eligible for parole until 2037 when I am 57 years old.

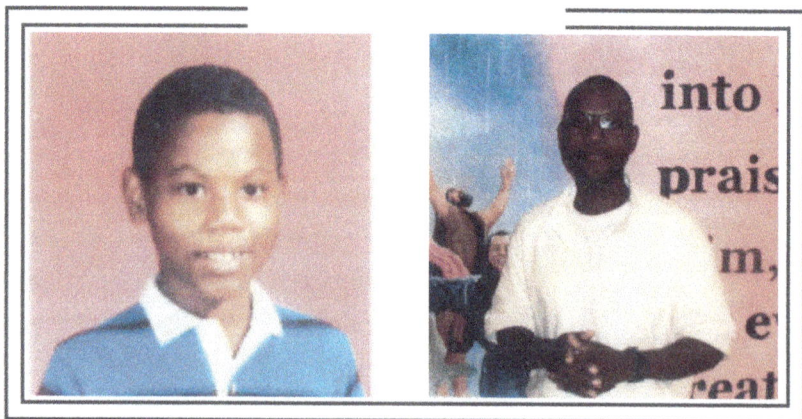

Anthony,

First things first, don't be quick to think you understand the world. Understanding the world takes time and mastery.

In past times, an apprentice worked 10,000 hours to be considered a master. I know you want to be relevant...to matter...but that comes through being a lifelong learner and much practice. There is a huge gulf between proficiency and mastery; surface conclusions over in-depth understanding. Only through exploration, can you fully live, thrive, and create your legacy.

As you start this journey: Create an atmosphere where this goal becomes the center of your focus. Occupy your thoughts, time, talk, concentration, persistence, and inner circle with seeking to understand.

Don't accept surface-level information and believe it is enough. Be aware of what you think you know...versus what you actually understand. Both externally...and internally. Habits and thoughts come from unexpected origins within ourselves. A wise man takes time to evaluate his motives and reasons. Self-reflection prevents us from acting in haste and rest assured, after practice, changes will occur.

Whether the circumstance demands a telescope, microscope, or simple tint, life is full of history to consider. Were others successful, or did they fail? What was the long-term outcome? Social responsibility is not just classroom theory. The impact on our neighbors matters and there is wisdom in the boundaries our communities set. How will you choose to be seen?

Lastly, the Lord is man's true refuge. Christ is what brings true repentance and reconciliation with the Father of all. Worldly wisdom might sound good, but it is not godly. So, remember any man quoting the words of God without giving praise to Him is a wreck waiting to happen. Trust the Holy Bible; it is full of direction and practical insight.

I know at the moment you may be confused. This wisdom may all seem good, but not exactly what you are looking for. So, one last thought to leave you with that's easily remembered.

When an artist creates a work of art, it has a duality, both negative space and the actual artistic expression. For the public viewers to fully appreciate the piece, the artist must learn composition and how to navigate the audience's focus.

You have skills and potential, but you are dwelling only on the negative space. I know you are just 11. I know Daddy just died, and you are numb. But please pay close attention to the negative space, as that defines the actual expression. You cannot have light without dark. Read Romans 8:28-29...or even the whole book of Romans...help is coming, hold on.

Stay up,

Love ya, little man,

Anthony Lewis

Merely Human

If you were to hear my voice
You may ask me, do I sing?
In response I'd ask, are you sure?
You can endure the sorrow this may bring
If my soul cries a lifetime filled with regrets
Though I may briefly find it to be worth living as melodious
    words paint melanism's imagery with its depths of
    expansive gambits urging one to hallowed ends
I will try to find Madam Maya in eternity because I have
    learned why the caged bird sings
How can an anguished soul envision liberation?
When even their dreams are no longer free
You'll come to find the answer lies within
My heart's rhapsody
Singing its story to me

ACCOMPLISHMENTS

- **Education:** A.A., Liberal Arts (Alvin Community College), A.A., Small Business Management (Ashworth Community College), GED (Windham School District)
- **Programs/Certificates:** Experiencing God, Bridges to Life, Battlefield of the Mind, Faith-Based Dorm, Cognitive Intervention, Disciples Prayer Life, Master Life, Celebrate Recovery, Heart of the Problem, Celebration Recovery, New Converts, Heart of the Problem (Facilitator), Battlefield of the Mind (Facilitator), Alpha, Anger Management, Christian Marriage Skills, Sense of Family, Husbands Seeking God, Purpose Driven Life (Facilitator), Peer Health / Safe Prison Training Program, Disciples Prayer Life (Facilitator), Peer Health, TASP Test, Technology Classes (Intro Computer Technology, Intro Computer Maintenance, Micro Computer Architecture, Computer System Maintenance, Computer System Peripherals, Computer Technology Networking, Computer System Troubleshooting), Paralegal Certificate (Blackstone Institute), Toastmasters International (1st Place Speech Contest, Competent Gavelier, Advance Gavelier Bronze, Advance Gavelier Silver), Regulation CFR Forklift Safety Operation Training Program, Birkman Career Management Test, Victim Advocacy (Adam State University), National Tax Training School
- **Work/On-the-Job Training:** Computer Peripheral Equipment Operator, Technical Drafting, Mechanical Drafting, Basic Computer Aid Drafting, Solid Model Design Drafting, Production Clerk, Stock Clerk, General Clerk, Forklift License, Alteration Tailor, Washing Machine Operator, Accountant Clerk
- **Other:** Baptism

28

MATT CARPENTER

I'm Matt Carpenter. I was incarcerated in June 2001, at the age of 17. I received 60 years as a plea bargain. I have served 19 years so far and am 36 years old. Under current legislation, I won't be eligible for parole until June 2031. By then I will be 47 and have served 30 years.

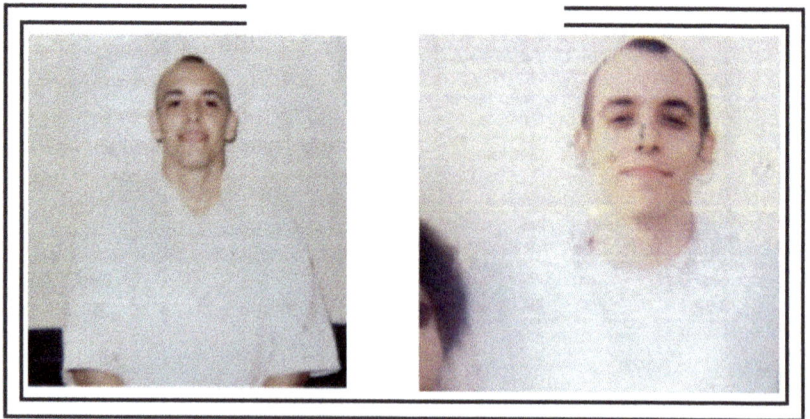

Dear Younger Self,

Wow! You are this little skinny ball of rage. You are young, confused, and angry. You hate your life and I get it.

Your parents split up when you were four. After a short stay with your grandparents, your mom took you and your brother to live with her new boyfriend, a very sour and cruel alcoholic. You can't understand why this man hates you.

He and your mom work long hours, but you all are still very poor. You live in a rundown trailer that happens to be in the district of a small middle upper-class school. This is not a good thing in your eyes.

You get bullied because you are poor, and your drunk stepdad is rude to other parents of kids who might befriend you. You are ashamed of your poverty and embarrassed of your parents, so you avoid most social gatherings like sports. You learn to be hateful, cruel, and a bully.

You need to realize that all of this is not about you. Don't take it so personally. Learn to read situations and the people involved. When teachers are dismissive of you, it doesn't mean they don't like you. And if they don't like you, that is their problem, not yours.

You are smart and good at school, but you lose interest because you don't have the money to participate in other areas. You show off to make friends. Attention is not admiration. You become known, but not popular. Realization of this only fuels your anger and disdain.

Stop wasting time trying to make people like you. Learn skills that can produce results, so that you won't have to resort to crime. Do you want to be popular, be useful? Skilled people make more money than drug dealers with less risk.

Do you think you are cool and tough because you hang out with older guys who have been in prison? Well, kid, the movies don't tell you about the hard metal stools, the slop that you eat every day, or how boring it is to waste your time endlessly. Trust me on this, you would rather be sitting in a plush CEO's chair writing checks than sitting on a hard stool writing lonely letters home. Steaks taste better than prison food. Your older self wishes he was hanging out with businessmen, politicians, and people that make a difference. To do that you need to work hard and have faith.

You also need to think about your family. Prison doesn't let you help them when they are in trouble. Prison doesn't let you go to kids' birthday parties. Prison doesn't care if you live hundreds of miles from home. Prison doesn't let you choose. And I know that would make you just as angry as you are now.

Learn that when you get angry and feel hopeless, there is a solution to every problem. Prison just puts more problems in front of your solution.

In everything, the reward is equal to the effort.

Your older self,

ACCOMPLISHMENTS

- **Education:** GED (Windham School District), on the waiting list for college
- **Programs/Certificates:** Walk Talk Peer Education, Discipleship Class, Peer Education Safe Prison, Cognitive Intervention Program, Bible Basic Class, Bridges to Life, OSHA Safety Training, Heat Illness Prevention
- **Work/On-the-Job Training:** Welding, Food Preparation, Warehouse Stock Clerk, Chemical Sanitation

29

OSCAR ORTIZ

Hello, my name is Oscar. In 1994, at the age of 17, I was sentenced to death. Later, in 1997, my death sentence was commuted to life and I thank God in his infinite wisdom and mercy for whatever reason it was put in the hearts of a second jury to spare my life. I have worked hard in this place toward becoming someone who is more than the sum of this environment. In May, I turned 44. Under current legislation, my first parole review will be in 2034.

Dear Oscar,

You're running. And, one day, you will get here.

Keep running.

One day you'll get here. Every day you'll get a dry square of corn-bread, and enough food to keep you alive, to keep you working. Food that is always soft and tasteless, it will be like scooping slop into your mouth as you're rushed out of the chow hall.

If you keep on running, wanting so badly to "be" somebody, you are finally going to catch up and be nobody. You will be property, assigned a number and a function, just another cog that keeps this machine working. You'll lose whatever promise is left of being human.

If you could only understand that you still have time to stop; you don't have to keep on running. You are blind and scared, with no idea that you are about to scar the world with a pain that will never heal, that you will feel for the rest of your days.

One day, as you look down into the steel toilet, the reflection you see will be that of an old man, who sometimes forgets why he wants to be free, a lifetime of his own pain anchoring him inside a prison within a prison, alone.

You don't have to keep running.

I want you to understand the bigness of life and of love. You are about to take that away from so many people. I want you to wake up to how close you are to the point of no return. I'd like to mentor you on the meaning and value of decisions, and how they influence the direction of your future, affecting all in your circumference. You need to be decisive and also capable of understanding that some things are too much to take on alone.

Already living on the streets at 16, I know you're afraid of turning back and unable to get a grip on the present. I want to give you a message of hope. Anyone, at any age, can self-destruct when running on autopilot. But, no one has to. So, please, let someone help you.

Stop running.

And trust someone to help you find your way back home. Be a son. Be a brother. And, one day you'll even be a real dad. But, right now you're young. No matter how you feel, you're not grown. But, you are a good person. And you're smart, with so much potential ahead of you.

There are a lot of people praying for you.

So, please, stop running, and let one of them help you to find your way home.

In prayer and faith, I am you at 44 and I hope that we never meet,

Oscar Ortiz

ACCOMPLISHMENTS

- **Education:** A.A., Small Business Management (Trinity Valley Community College)
- **Programs/Certificates:** Paralegal Certificate Course (University of Houston-Center for Advanced Management Programs), Small Business Management (Trinity Valley Community College), Faith Formation Course (Knights of Columbus), "We Believe" Catholic Home Study Course, Basic Catholic Catechists Course
- **Work/On-the-Job Training:** Cook, Alteration Tailor, Officer's Dining Room
- **Other:** Baptism, Phi Theta Kappa Honor Society, Confraternity of the Most Holy Rosary, Militia Immaculate (Moderator), Knights at the Foot of the Cross

30

LIZANNA RAMIREZ

M y name is Lizanna Ramirez, and I am currently serving a 75-year sentence for murder. This tragedy happened when I was 17 years of age, and I am now 41 years old. I have served 23 years so far. Under current legislation, I won't be eligible for parole until 2026.

Lizanna,

There's no way you can grasp this right now, but you are NOT a mistake. God designed you exactly the way you are, unique and different.

Later in life, you'll understand that parents aren't perfect and they're trying to figure out life with their own issues and flaws. I wish I could tell you that you won't always feel lost, abandoned and rejected. It won't always be this way. But the instability at home will determine a lot of the choices you make. Feeling unloved, you'll find security with a group of guys who allow you to feel safe and accepted in your own identity. The world will be cruel to you because of the way you look and you, in turn, are cruel back because of your own hurts turned into anger. Experiences will be your number one teacher throughout trials and hurt.

You'll be in and out of juvenile detention centers (not knowing that God is trying to get your attention and slow you down). Because you desire acceptance from a group of guys who are like family, you'll try to prove to them that you're just as strong as they are and deserving of the love and respect they give to you.

I wish I could stop you from the dark path you're headed toward, but you will discover at the tender age of 12 that you have a God-given talent to cut hair, even with no license, and your skills will attract attention. You have the ability and character to make people laugh, despite your painful upbringing. You will accept people for who they are no matter what they look like because you know the pain of not being accepted.

You have no idea now, but at the age of 17, you will be charged for murder. When you find yourself alone in that cell, you'll finally cry out to God, pleading with Him to help you and forgive you...and at that moment, you will carry his life on your heart...but God who forgives has forgiven you.

You will accept your time and you'll tell yourself, "I will learn to be better. I'll try my best to grow up from here on out." You'll tell yourself that everything you've gone through was to help bring out a better and bigger purpose for God's glory. Piece by piece, you'll see that all the hurt brought you to a place where you leaned completely on God. He loves you just the way you are. He will heal you from feeling abandoned, rejected and unloved. God will bring your family back to you, and they will learn how to love you just the way you've always wanted.

You see, it's taken 23 years to gain this perspective and wisdom because, at 17, I came from a single parent who was an addict and an older sister who didn't want me around. I sought affection elsewhere and lost myself even more until I landed in prison. Not all of my time has been wasted, as the fruits of adversity, isolation and suffering have been a changed heart, even after so many years of incarceration. There are still many things to be gained from my circumstances such as the opportunity to tell my story to offer encouragement and help others to find meaning in their lives. In some ways, people can draw strength and inspiration from my story when they see my hope. That is satisfying.

I pray that when I come out of here, I'm an asset to my family and society, that I'm an example that broken people can heal and have value. I've learned to be productive and that life is all about relationships. I see the bigger picture now.

Thank you for listening and God bless.

Truly,

Lizann Ramirez

ACCOMPLISHMENTS

- **Programs/Certificates:** Bridges to Life, Celebrate Recovery, Hope in the Storm, Voyager, Overcomers, New Beginnings
- **Work/On-the-Job Training:** Warehouseman, Forklift, Cook, Stock Clerk, Microcomputer Specialist, Washing Machine Operator, Alteration Tailor, Carpentry Fundamentals

31

JUAN ANTONIO RODRIGUEZ

My name is Juan Antonio Rodriguez. I was 16 years old when I was arrested in December 1993. In February 1994, I was certified as an adult and transferred from juvenile court to the adult court system. In July 1994, I was sentenced to life in prison. Under current legislation, I must serve 30 calendar years before I am eligible for parole. I am 42 years old and have been incarcerated for 26 years now. My parole eligibility date is February 18, 2024.

Dear Little Tony,

I pray and hope you have an open mind and some kind of understanding while reading this letter. You are hurting because you miss Dad very much and wish he were still alive. Please listen to what I'm about to tell you and take my advice to heart.

Stop hanging around troublemakers – they don't make you look cool. If you keep associating with them, then sooner or later you will end up in an unfortunate situation that will cause serious pain to the people who love and care for you.

How are you going to feel knowing Mom is crying because of something you did? Do you want to see Mom cry? Are you still going to think you are cool when you go to juvenile detention and Mom comes to see you crying? Surely that's not what you want.

Don't take life and family for granted. You need to appreciate that you are alive, healthy, and have a family who cares for you and loves you very much. Remember that your actions affect many people's lives, not just your own. Appreciate the countless sacrifices Mom makes just to make you happy.

What do you want to do or become when you grow up? What will help you achieve your goals? First, you must stop hanging around troublemakers. Second, please take school more seriously and pass all of your classes. If you want to become a boxing champion, that will require intense training, discipline, and a strict diet. Believe in yourself, stay out of trouble and finish school.

Most importantly, you need God in your life. Without Him, nothing is possible. He needs to be prioritized before anything and everything. Go to church and ask for His guidance, protection, mercy, and forgiveness of your sins.

You may not comprehend everything I'm telling you in this letter because you haven't been placed in juvenile detention yet. You can't grasp the pain and suffering you will cause by ending up there. However, if you keep hanging around those troublemakers, that's exactly where you will find yourself. Do you want to break Mom's heart and make her cry? Of course, you don't. Please make Mom proud.

I pray this letter changes your thinking before you make a major mistake that you will regret for the rest of your life. Trust me, you don't want to live in regret. Take my advice and please listen to Mom.

Sincerely,

Juan "Jony" Rodriguez

ACCOMPLISHMENTS

- **Education:** GED (Windham School District), Electronic Trade, College Computer Repair Trade
- **Programs/Certificates:** Peer Health Education Course, numerous Emmaus Correspondence School certificates, Cognitive Intervention, OSHA Industry Safety
- **Work/On-the-Job Training:** Manufacturer, Agribusiness and Logistics – Sandblaster and Shear Operator

32

RICHARD EDWIN SMITH

I am Richard Edwin Smith. At 16, I was sentenced to 99 years in prison for my role in a murder. I've been incarcerated for 30 years. In February 2020, I was approved for parole. I will live out the rest of my life making myself into a better person to serve the needs of others.

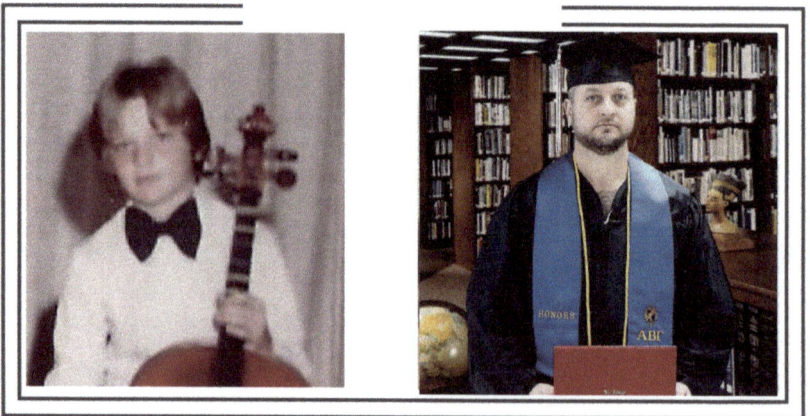

Dear Self,

I'll begin by saying you are a smart, talented, and greatly loved young man. When Mom and Dad tell you these things, listen to them. A wonderful life awaits you if you embrace who you are. When I was your age, I didn't.

As a youth, I believed I could do whatever I desired. No matter the consequences, I thought it would all get straightened up later. I thought I could act up until I was 18, flip a switch, and then act right. My "18 opportunity" never came.

At 16, I was involved in an inexcusable offense (murder) that got me sentenced to 99 years in prison. Thirty long years later, I've been serving out that sentence. One senseless decision will haunt me forever. There is no closure when someone's life is taken. There are no "do-overs" in the game of life.

Right now you are brave, curious, and adventurous. You have a full life of spectacular success laid out before you. No task is too daunting, no challenge too hard. You are made for great things. But don't get it twisted. Just because you can, doesn't mean you should. Some things are not meant to be done. Drugs are one of them.

At the beginning of drug use, you may think it is fun. Does it make you cool or tough? No. That's a lie sent straight from the pit of Hell! Drugs will make you into a broken shadow of who you once were. They will rob you of any chance of becoming who you are meant to be.

When I increased my drug use, my lifestyle shifted to one of crime. I lived in the selfish pursuit of my desires. If I hurt someone else in the process, I didn't care. Somehow that little boy who was kind and caring became a mean-spirited stranger. It was only years later that this became evident.

When it did, I realized I was guilty of causing ever-widening ripples of despair. My selfishness ruined others' lives. I lived with shame, bitterness, and regret over my parts in unspeakable horrors. Once a crime is committed, nobody remains unchanged.

Before you step off the cliff, please know you have a heart of gold. Don't corrupt it by seeking acceptance from others. Their approval is not what you need. You need to be who you are, not who others want you to be. Walk in love and compassion. Don't be the problem, be the solution.

As I've said, I've done things that I deeply regret. Those things serve as daily reminders of the person I wish I never became. "How could I?" haunts my dreams. "If only" reawakens the ache in my heart for a "do-over" that will never come.

I cannot change the past, but I hope with every fiber of my being that you will take heed to this letter so that my present will never become your future. I'll spend the rest of my life making amends for what I've done. Although I can change on my own, it is God who can truly transform a life as lost as mine. I urge you to turn to Him before you go astray. Live as a beacon of hope even in the darkest of situations. The cycle of insanity must be broken, and it starts with you.

I plead with you to not throw away your life with a slew of terrible decisions. Don't try to clean up a disaster when you can avoid the disaster. Live your life in such a way that you will never regret a deed done nor a word said. Live a life of love.

You are greater than you now realize. Embrace that fact.

Much love,

Richard Smith

ACCOMPLISHMENTS

- **Education:** A.A.S., Welding Technology and A.A.S. Business Management (Lee College; Magna Cum Laude)
- **Programs/Certificates:** Volunteer Tutor (Windham School District Welding School; Lee College Welding; Lee College Academics), Faith-Based Dorm (Facilitator), House Church (Program Trainer/Facilitator), Leadership School of Transformation (Facilitator/Group Leader), Life Change Group (Facilitator for G4 Offenders), Mike Barber Ministries (Weekend Setup Crew), Emmaus Walk (Servant), Kairos (Inside Coordinator), Paralegal Certification, Real Estate Law Specialty Course, Civil Litigation Specialty Course (Professional Career Development Institute), Toastmasters International (Wynne Gavel Club, Former Club President, Competent Communicator Award), Theater Group (Co-Director), Leadership School of Transformation (Revival Group Pastor), ASE Certified Technician (Medium/Heavy Truck Technician – T2 Diesel Engines, T4 Brakes, T6), Automobile Technician (A5 Brakes, A6 Electrical/Electronic Systems)
- **Work/On-the-Job Training:** Teacher's Aide (Windham School District, Diesel Mechanics School), Rockwell Chapel Sound Crew, Furniture Factory, Electronics Mechanic (Maintenance Department), Diesel Mechanics School, Teacher's Aide, Shop Diagnostician, Diesel Technician, Create/Maintain Shop Forms and Records Using Microsoft Office
- **Other:** *Echo* prison newspaper contributing writer; published memoir *God Don't Lie* (Christian Faith Publishing), various magazine articles in *Redeemed, Air Boating, Slab, Bayou Review, Alpha Beta Gamma* (Business Honor Society, Delta Sigma Chapter)

33

JAMAL ANTWAN REED

My name is Jamal A. Reed, and I have been incarcerated since 1995. I was 17 years old after I was certified as an adult at the age of 16, in 1994. I was given two 80-year sentences that are running concurrently. As of this point in time I have been incarcerated for 25 years. Under current standards of legislation, I have to complete a total of 30 calendar years before I am eligible for parole in the year 2025, at age 47. If I am then granted parole, I would then have to start and complete a separate three year prison sentence that I foolishly picked up as a juvenile while in TDCJ. My release date for this portion of my prison sentence has not been determined.

Jamal,

Within my first five years in prison, I have had to endure much emotional pain with the loss of many loved ones, including my mother. Once my mother passed away, I remembered what an officer told me once within my first year in prison. He said, "You have a lot of prison time; what are you going to do when your mother and everyone else passes away?" I began to think about myself without a family or support for the length of my prison sentence. The beginning of an eye-opener for me.

Once I am released from prison, I will be very confused and scared being that I don't have the support as so many and the fact that I don't know how to properly job hunt or do taxes, etc. Nor do I know if I will have relatives still living to help me reintegrate back into society. I think this was one of the hardest things that I had to do because I didn't know how to start this letter, better yet a conversation to myself. To write a random juvenile a letter, I believe, would have been a whole lot easier.

It is true to me that hindsight is 20/20 and when sitting down and reflecting on the paths taken which led me to prison. I didn't listen to my mother every time that she told me in my preteens that "I didn't need any friends," and "I wasn't grown so stop trying to be." I brought these two quotes to light because if I could tell myself then what I know now, it would be that peer pressure is a real thing that will dictate the present and future if not assessed properly.

I now know about peer pressure in a way you don't understand. I've believed that I could help fix any minor living issues of being the male of the house and protecting my mother with no father in the household. You feel the need to be the protector and the man of the house. Because your rational thinking became distorted, you believed that you could choose who you wanted to associate with or be friends with and no one could tell you otherwise. Just because you are getting older and bigger doesn't mean you're a "man."

Listen to your mother. She knows the best type of people to associate with or not to. She has the experience because she had seven siblings, and she was once young. It's okay to sit down, take the time to first listen to the elder family members' advice. Think about what they said and do the simple right thing that you have been told to do. Your mother and family love and care for you. They don't want you to get hurt, killed, or in trouble. Your joy is her happiness.

You'll make better choices if you don't allow peer pressure, distractions, or fear dictate your present path to the future. To be a kid is important. Your mind is not yet properly developed. Many men are trapped in their minds and bodies. That is not a good thing or way to live life. You may come to regret a lot of decisions and choices you make. The important thing is that you are the author of your story. You are a writer and producer. Make good decisions.

Because of these things, I've personally learned to get a grip on my life and gain perspective. I have realized past decisions and actions do not define us; they only dictate our future. If you accept the knowledge you are given, you can have the life you want, instead of this life I'm now living.

I regret the paths I've taken, but love who I've met along the way through my recovery. Jesus Christ is my Lord and Savior.

Jamal A. Reed

ACCOMPLISHMENTS

- **Education:** GED (Windham School District), A.A., Liberal Arts (Alvin Community College), Vocational Trade of Computer Repair (Alvin Community College)
- **Programs/Certificates:** Toastmasters International, Anger Management, Men's Fraternity, OSHA safety training
- **Work/On-the-Job Training:** Furniture Factory, Janitorial Services, Laundry Cleaning, Food Service, Agriculture, Barber, Forklift Operator, Boiler Room Operator, Door Lock Mechanic
- **Other:** Church, Bible Study

34

JACQUE ARMAND WILSON

M y name is Jacque Wilson. I was the age of 15, and incarcerated in the year of 1993, being prescribed a capital life sentence of 35 flat calendar years. As of this present moment I've been incarcerated approximately 26 years, 9 months, and I'm 42 years old. Eligibility for parole will be the year of 2028.

Dear Jacque,

Greetings to you, young man. All praise and glory to our Lord and Savior Jesus Christ. Jacque, allow me to share with you what led me to prison. In my younger years I desperately wanted to be accepted. I hung with the wrong group of guys with whom I ended up making a poor decision, partaking in a robbery that was only to scare but ended in the death of a man who was someone's son, brother, husband, uncle, best friend, mentor.

Had I known what I know now, for example, how important it is to trust God first and foremost, things may have been different. I would've watched less TV and spent more time reading, exploring the world through the different writings of authors who shared similar childhoods, and taking my education more seriously which would contribute to my future.

What I would like to say to you is take your time growing up, absorb all the education you can, and surround yourself with people who will correct you whenever you're in error instead of those who will just agree with everything you say and do or lead you into darkness (arrested development).

Here are some levels of growth that have shaped me into the man I've become today. Communication is a major tool. You need to understand others, share your feelings, express love, care, and concern, build relationships, and fellowship with brothers and sisters in Christ. That was one major tool I wish I had used in my younger years.

You will be experiencing many changes (life lessons with adversity) which will contribute to the shaping of your character, self-esteem, understanding of self. There will be many people God puts on your life path who are there to warn you, edify, motivate, and inspire you to become a better person each day you live. Don't become flippant or take this for granted.

If you've wronged someone – correct that, take ownership and responsibility for your actions. Be mindful of the words you speak because there is power in them to build up or destroy. Never be afraid of change because it's very beneficial in life. Spend some time journaling, taking inventory of yourself. By doing so, you'll be surprised at the many things you have an interest in, and untapped potential will surface.

Whenever you feel like a failure, try again and take more steps. You will succeed. Show your love in actions, stay focused on you, and never become distracted by what others are doing. Keep God at the center of your life more than anything. Your future largely depends on what you learn and practice from this moment onward. Knowledge is power, and there is no power greater than knowledge of self. Where we are lacking self-knowledge, we are lacking power to change. Take care of yourself, may God bless you.

Your matured self,

Jacque Wilson

ACCOMPLISHMENTS

- **Programs/Certificates:** Wellness Integrated Balanced Living Course, Study Guide Correspondence Course (The Amazing Facts Bible School), Voyager, Handling Suppression Course, Peer Health Education Course, The Personal Integrity Course, The Learning Skills Course, The Overcoming Addiction Course, The Successful Parenting Course (Criminon), Leadership Course, The Communication Tools Course, The Conditions Of Life Course, Christian Studies, Core Curriculum Introductory Craft Skills, Torah Club's Unrolling The Scroll (Vol.1-Genesis, Exodus, Leviticus, Numbers, Deuteronomy), HaYesod Program (Christianity And Its Jewish Roots), OSHA Construction Safety, Kairos, Christian Studies In Methods Of Bible Study, One-Year-Long Step-Study (Commitment to Spiritual Healing from All Hurts, Habits, Hang-Ups, and Addictions), Focus On The Family's Truth Project
- **Work/On-the-Job Training:** Cook, Carpentry Level One, Curricular Industrial Maintenance Level One, Construction Fundamentals, Construction Carpentry, Construction Site Safety Orientation

35

CARSON LEE WILLIAMS

M y name is Carson and I eagerly write this to share with you about myself, who I was, who I am, and who I continue to strive to be. I am 43 years old and I have been incarcerated since 1994, at the age of 17. It will be another four years before I will be eligible for parole (2024). By that time. I will have served 30 years for the misgiving of youth. The fortuitous benefit of me being here has allowed me to grow, learn, and become productive.

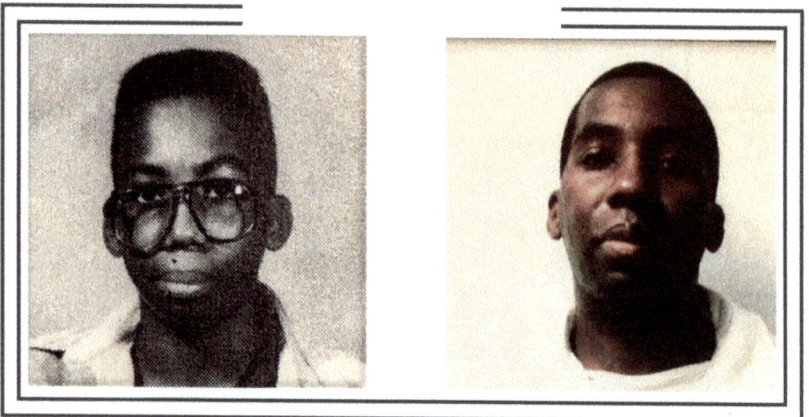

Dear Carson,

I know going through all that physical abuse from your father and brother wasn't easy. Holding all that in for years built up so much anger inside. I realize why your temper was so bad. Mom wasn't home much because she was always working so she could provide for her two boys. You were always moving from place to place and kept changing schools.

Even though I went through a lot growing up, my lack of knowledge of what it takes to be a man is what led me to prison. Manhood is about setting examples through your behavior, facing personal and collective problems honestly, and working to alleviate them. Finally, manhood involves knowing the difference between right and wrong and refusing to substitute excuses and expediency for what is right. Too many of your peers believe that in the attempt to get what they want, anything goes.

Well, it doesn't.

The price paid for this attitude is far greater than if you would simply do what is right and just. Let me share with you what kind of men we need in this world: men who are willing to stand, step up for principle, are honest as the day is long, decent, full of truth and morality, and respond to their conscience even when it is unpopular to do so. We need men who know there is something within that is not open for negotiation—that bribery cannot touch, questionable friends cannot influence, nor money can buy. We need men who are willing to stand for virtue and high standards in a world where indifference and indecency slowly rule the day. We need men who will not waver in the face of doubt, personify excellence, hold a vision of what can be and not what was. We need spirit-filled men who are love-abiding sons of the Most High. We need men who will teach their children about the God they serve. We need men who will kneel in prayer rather than stand in frustration.

Basketball wasn't "it" for you. Basketball wasn't your triumph. You are more than basketball. You are more than a game. More than a player in someone's gym. You had a more important future in store for yourself.

When it comes to the resilience of the human spirit, sometimes you've got to approach life with a zero-tolerance policy toward self-pity. When things go wrong, when the whole world seems against you, you have to stop and realize: this is my life now. This is where you're at. Now what?

It's up to you to choose what you do with the situation. By eliminating self-pity and replacing it with self-empowerment, we can move forward. You can't change what has happened but you can change how you allow it to affect you and what you choose to do moving forward. When you would get angry or feel those negative vibes, it wasn't "you." It was your reaction to your physical condition. And yet, you allowed those situations to direct your emotional well-being. You can no longer allow those experiences to govern the way you feel. Looking back, I'm not sure you would have made it if it weren't for the angels God placed on this earth for you and the tools they gave you.

"To evolve, one must not be involved."

You have to find more effective ways of dealing with the unpleasantness and horrors of your circumstances so you can find your peace. In your darkest moments, you discovered your light. You didn't have to search for it. No one handed it to you. It was there. In you. The whole time. You just had to rediscover it.

You are not dead, even though sometimes it feels that you are. You are very much alive. A few things should immediately become clear. You have choices. Success comes to no one; you have to go get it.

Very sincerely,

Carson Williams

ACCOMPLISHMENTS

- **Education:** GED (Windham School District)
- **Programs/Certificates:** HIV Peer Educator Training, Peer
  Health and Sexual Assault Awareness, Friendship Ministry
  Bible Study (Series: Introduction, Grace, Salvation, Jonah,
  Contrast, Overcoming, Deity of Jesus, Holy Spirit, Friendship,
  Understanding the Enemy), Faith-Based Classes (What on
  Earth Am I Here For), The Bait of Satan, The Quest for
  Authentic Manhood, The Truth Protect, Faith-Based Program,
  Acceleron Learning (Family Health, Career Planning, Financial
  Literacy, Workplace Skills), Wild at Heart Boot Camp (Trinity
  Fellowship Church)

ACKNOWLEDGMENTS

As with any endeavor of great significance, it takes a community of passionate people to pursue such a vision.

To all of the Second Lookers and the Epicenter Family, this book is dedicated to you. We are humbled by your support, encouragement, and desire to show Texas that children are more than their worst mistake.

With deep gratitude we thank:

Emma DeCaro, Epicenter's Communications Director, for compiling the content and spearheading the project along with your friends (Danielle Jones, Susan Aiello, Bianca Rivera, Rebekah Brooks, Karamee English, and Raquel Rodriguez) and former English teachers (Martha Medlock and Marilyn DuVon) who helped us type, edit and review each letter. This project would not have been possible without the sacrifice and the endless hours you contributed;

Carolyn Bullard for your assistance with the final polish and editing;

Chon Dimas and Reaz Ahmed, Epicenter Advisory Board members, for putting our vision to paper and formatting the project;

All the Second Look authors for your willingness to share your heart-felt words, without which, this project would not have been possible;

Alex Luprete for creating the moving Second Look video and messaging that would inspire the vision for the book;

Terran Washington for jumping in at the last minute and designing the amazing cover for the book;

Jaime Long and Cyntoia Brown Long for sharing your enthusiasm for the Second Look Movement and Cyntoia specifically for sharing your own "Word to My Younger Self."

Lindsey Linder for your contribution to the book, your tenacity, and constant support for Second Look;

Chris Self, Epicenter's Chief Counsel, for your insightful examination of the Texas Board of Pardons and Paroles;

Jasmine Bond and Lindsay West for giving us a detailed overview of the Texas Law of Parties and how the law affects juveniles;

Jodi Thompson of Fawkes Press for guiding us through the publishing process;

And the Epicenter Ministries volunteer board and staff members for all you do to keep things rolling.

Most importantly, to God be the glory, for through Him, all things are possible.

DEANNA LUPRETE

FOUNDING EXECUTIVE DIRECTOR, EPICENTER MINISTRIES

LEAH METZLER

CHIEF OF STAFF, EPICENTER MINISTRIES

In Memory of
Trevon Toney
August 8, 2000 – May 19, 2020

"Jesus wept."
John 11:35 (ESV)

NOTES

Introduction to Second Look at the Texas Legislature

1. SEE GENERALLY, S. Johnson, R. Blum, and J. Giedd, *Adolescent Maturity and the Brain: The Promise and Pitfalls of Neuroscience Research in Healthy Policy*, Journal of Adolescent Health, Volume 45(3), (Sept. 2009).
2. *Roper v. Simmons*, 543, U.S. 551, 470 (2005).
3. *Miller v. Alabama*, 132 S.Ct. (2012).
4. ACLU, *At America's Expense: The Mass Incarceration of the Elderly*, June 2012, https:www.aclu.org/files/assets/elderlyprisonreport_20120613_1.pdf Calculation = ((Average cost per year per inmate to incarcerate before age 50 x 34) + (National estimate for annual cost for the care of an inmate after age 50 x 21)).
5. Ibid. Calculation = (Average cost per year per inmate to incarcerate before age 50 x 20).

An Introduction to Texas Parole

1. Parole/Mandatory Supervision Information: Approval/Denial Reasons, Texas Bd. of Pardons & Paroles, https://www.tdcj.texas.gov/bpp/what_is_parole/reasons.htm (last accessed Feb. 14, 2020).
2. Jolie McCollough, *A judge told Texas to put some inmates in air conditioning. Lawyers say prison officials are violating that order*, Texas Tribune, September 5, 2019, https://www.texastribune.org/2019/09/05/texas-prison-air-conditioning-heat-contempt-motion/ (last accessed Feb. 14, 2020).
3. Vicky Camarillo, *The Penal System Today is Slavery: Lawmakers Finally Start to Talk About Unpaid Labor in Texas Prisons*, Texas Observer, May 10, 2019, https://texasobserver.org/penal-system-slavery-unpaid-labor-texas/ (last accessed Feb. 14, 2020).
4. Jolie McCullough, *Three Texas inmates have died at the hands of prison officers as use of fore continues to rise*, Texas Tribune, Feb. 7, 2020, https://www.texastribune.org/2020/02/07/texas-prison-deaths-come-staffers-use-force-against-inmates-increases/ (last accessed Feb. 14, 2020).
5. Evelyn Patterson, *The Dose-Response of Time Served in Prison on Mortality: New York State*, 1989-2003, American Journal of Public Health 103, no. 3 (March 1, 2013): pp. 523-528.
6. Texas Bd. of Pardons & Paroles, *Instructions for Completing the Texas Bd. of Pardons & Paroles Risk Assessment*, p. 2 (March 1, 2016); Texas Bd. of Pardons & Paroles, *Parole Guidelines Annual Report FY 2015*, p. 3 (Apr. 2016) (citing Standard Parole Guidelines, Board Rule 145.2(b)(1)).
7. Id.
8. Texas Sunset Advisory Commission, The Board of Pardon and Paroles: A Staff Report to the Sunset Advisory Commission 7 (1986) available online at https://

www.sunset.texas.gov/reviews-and-reports/agencies/board-pardons-andparoles-bpp (last accessed Nov. 13, 2016).

9. *Ruiz v. Estelle*, 503 F. Supp. 1265 (S.D. Tex. 1980).

10. Texas Sunset Advisory Commission, Staff Report: Texas Department of Criminal Justice, Board of Pardons and Paroles, Correctional Managed Health Care Committee 26 (2006) available online at https://www.sunset.texas.gov/reviews-and-reports/agencies/board-pardons-and-paroles-bpp (last accessed Nov. 13, 2016).

11. Waterman, Alan, *Identity Development from Adolescence to Adulthood*, 18 DEVELOP-MENTAL PSYCHOL. 341, 355 (1982).

12. Steinberg, Laurence, *Should the Science of Adolescent Brain Development Inform Public Policy?*, 64 AM. PSYCHOL. 739-750 (2009).

13. *Roper v. Simmons*, 543 U.S, 551 (2005); *Graham v. Florida*, 560 U.S. 48 (2010); *Miller v. Alabama*, 567 U.S. 460 (2012).

14. American Civil Liberties Union, *"False Hope: How Parole Systems Fail Youth Serving Extreme Sentences,"* 6 (2016).

15. For the previously introduced version, see 2019 Texas House Bill No. 256 (NS), Texas Eighty-Sixth Legislature.

16. Bryan Stevenson, *Just Mercy: A Story of Justice and Redemption*. First edition. New York: Spiegel & Grau, 2015.

Juveniles & the Law of Parties

1. Tex. Pen. Code. §7.01.

2. Tex. Pen. Code §7.02(a)(1).

3. Tex. Pen. Code §7.02(a)(3).

4. Tex. Pen. Code §7.02(a)(2).

5. *Miller v. Alabama*, 567 U.S 460 (2012) citing *Roper v. Simmons*, 543 U.S. 551 (2005).

6. Steinberg, Laurence & Monahan, Kathryn, *Age Differences in Resistance to Peer Influence* 43 DEVELOPMENTAL PSYCHOL. 1531-1543 (2007).

7. Chein, Jason , Albert, Dustin, O'Brien, Lia, Uckert, Kaitlyn & Steinberg, Laurence *Peers Increase Adolescent Risk Taking by Enhancing Activity in the Brain's Reward Circuitry* 14 DEVELOPMENTAL SCIENCE. 1-10 (2011).

8. Cauffman, Elizabeth & Steinberg, Laurence *Emerging Findings from Research on Adolescent Development and Juvenile Justice* 7 AM. PSYCHOL. 428-449 (2012).

9. Spear, Linda Patria, *The Adolescent Brain and Age-Related Behavioral Manifestations*, 24 NEOROSCI. & BIOBEHAV. REVS. 417, 421 (2000).

10. Scott, Elizabeth & Steinberg, Laurence *Adolescent Development and the Regulation of Youth Crime. The Future of Children* 18 AM. PSYCHOL. 15-33 (2008).

11. Steinberg, Laurence, *Should the Science of Adolescent Brain Development Inform Public Policy?*, 64 AM. PSYCHOL. 739–750 (2009).

12. Id.

13. Id.

14. Spear, Linda Patria, *The Adolescent Brain and Age-Related Behavioral Manifestations*, 24 NEOROSCI. & BIOBEHAV. REVS. 417, 421 (2000).

15. Id.

16. Scott, Elizabeth & Steinberg, Laurence *Adolescent Development and the Regulation of Youth Crime. The Future of Children* 18 AM. PSYCHOL. 15-33 (2008).

17. Steinberg, Laurence *A Social Neuro-Science Perspective of Adolescent Risk-Taking* 28 DEV REV 78-106 (2008).

18. Johnson, Sarah, Blum, Robert & Cheng, Tina *Future Orientation: A Construct with Implications for Adolescent Health and Well-Being* 26 INT J ADOLESC MED HEALTH 459-466 (2014).

19. Moffit, Terrie *Adolescence-Limited and Life-Course-Persistent Antisocial Behavior: A Developmental Taxonomy* 100 PSYCHOL. REV 674-701 (1993).

20. Lipsey, M.W., Howell, J.C., Kelly, M.R., Chapman, G., and Carver, D., *Improving the Effectiveness of Juvenile Justice Programs A New Perspective on Evidence-Based Practice.* (2010), https://cjjr.georgetown.edu/wp-content/uploads/2015/03/ImprovingEffectiveness_December2010.pdf.

21. *Correctional Education Guidance Package*, U.S. Dept. of Edu. (May 21, 2020), http://www2.ed.gov/policy/gen/guid/correctional-education/fact-sheet.pdf.

22. Steinberg, Laurence & Monahan, Kathryn, *Age Differences in Resistance to Peer Influence* 43 DEVELOPMENTAL PSYCHOL. 1531-1543 (2007).

www.ingramcontent.com/pod-product-compliance
Lightning Source LLC
Chambersburg PA
CBHW041934260326
41914CB00010B/1296